This copy of

THE FACT-A-MINUTE BOOK
by Paul James

belongs to

_____

_____

THE
FACT-A-MINUTE
BOOK

Paul James

SPARROW
BOOKS

A Sparrow Book

Published by Arrow Books Limited
17–21 Conway Street, London W1P 5HL

An imprint of the Hutchinson Publishing Group

London Melbourne Sydney Auckland
Johannesburg and agencies
throughout the world

First published 1982
© Victorama Ltd, 1982

Set in Century Schoolbook
by Book Economy Services, Burgess Hill, Sussex

Made and printed in Great Britain
by the Anchor Press Ltd
Tiptree, Essex

ISBN 0 09 927360 8

00:00 There are 60 minutes in 1 hour, 1440 minutes in a day, and 527,040 minutes in a leap year.

00:01 You can tell the age of a fish by counting the rings on its scales, in the same way that you can tell the age of a tree by counting the rings through its trunk.

00:02 Marble Arch in London was built as an entrance to Buckingham Palace, until it was discovered that it was too narrow for a state coach to pass through.

00:03 Hens in the USA lay approximately 1,380,000 eggs every minute.

00:04 A shrew eats two thirds of its own weight every day.

00:05 The famous Eiffel Tower in Paris is held together with two and a half million rivets.

00:06 In Biblical times it was believed that the snake stung with its tail.

00:07 The longest word in the Oxford English Dictionary is FLOCCIPAUCINIHILIPILIFICATION. It means the action of estimating as worthless.

5

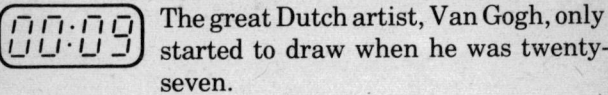 It has been proved that elephants do have good memories, and tests show that they have 73 to 100 per cent recall even after a year.

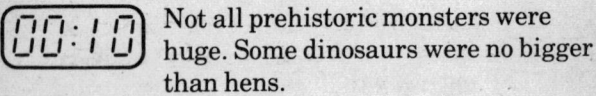 The great Dutch artist, Van Gogh, only started to draw when he was twenty-seven.

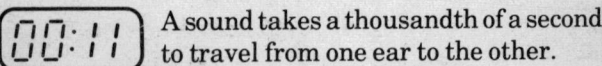 Not all prehistoric monsters were huge. Some dinosaurs were no bigger than hens.

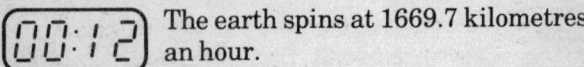 A sound takes a thousandth of a second to travel from one ear to the other.

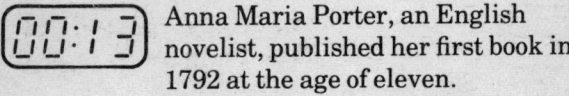 The earth spins at 1669.7 kilometres an hour.

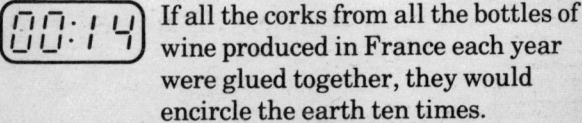 Anna Maria Porter, an English novelist, published her first book in 1792 at the age of eleven.

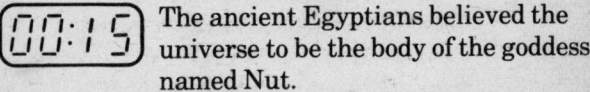 If all the corks from all the bottles of wine produced in France each year were glued together, they would encircle the earth ten times.

The ancient Egyptians believed the universe to be the body of the goddess named Nut.

For its size the lion has the smallest heart of all beasts of prey.

`00:17` The Mongolian rat survives in the desert without ever having a drink. It gets all the liquid it needs from its food.

`00:18` A large number of British women develop bunions before the age of forty.

`00:19` Moles are very strong swimmers.

`00:20` X-rays of the 'Mona Lisa' show that three totally different versions were painted.

`00:21` In Germany carp is eaten on New Year's Eve to bring good luck.

`00:22` Elderly bears take baths in sulphur springs to ease their pains.

`00:23` After his first concert appearance Elvis Presley was advised to become a lorry driver.

`00:24` An alligator's bellow can be heard a mile away.

`00:25` Anne Boleyn, the second wife of Henry VIII, spent the night before her execution in the same room in the Tower of London in which she spent the night before her coronation.

`00:26` Micro-organisms have been dug out of Antarctic ice, still alive after half a million years.

`00:27` In New Orleans every corpse is buried in a mausoleum because the ground is too damp for normal burial.

`00:28` The world's largest telescope was built in Russia in 1970. It is 80 feet long, weighs 935 tons, and can show objects 15,000 miles away.

`00:29` Britain has more ghosts per square mile than any other country.

`00:30` Boomerangs only fly back to the thrower if they miss their targets. Once a boomerang hits what it was aimed at it can't fly back.

`00:31` Bees dance to show other bees where they have found pollen.

`00:32` Enough hot-dogs are produced every year in America to reach the moon and back two and a half times.

`00:33` There is more sugar in a kilo of lemons than in a kilo of strawberries.

`00:34` Every minute in the world 238 people are born and 97 die.

`00:35` Dolphins sleep with one eye open.

`00:36` Robins eat the equivalent of fourteen feet of worms every day.

`00:37` There are twenty-seven words for 'snow' in the Eskimo language.

`00:38` The Hundred Years War actually lasted 114 years.

`00:39` There are approximately 800,000 words in the English language.

`00:40` Sea otters have two coats of fur.

`00:41` North American grizzly bears can run as fast as many horses.

`00:42` Gale warnings were first issued in 1861.

`00:43` A litre of vinegar is heavier in winter than in the summer.

`00:44` In County Durham in the North of England is a place called 'Pity Me'.

`00:45` Garlic belongs to the lily family.

`00:46` There are 4000 man-made objects flying about in outer space.

`00:47` The water from artesian wells in the Australian outback fell as rain 6000 years ago.

`00:48` The human body has 206 bones.

`00:49` Female ticks lay 5000 eggs at a time.

`00:50` An owl can consume as many as ten mice in a single meal.

`00:51` C. N. Swift wrote the Lord's Prayer twenty-five times on a piece of paper half the size of a postage stamp.

`00:52` Seals only fall asleep for intervals of one and a half minutes.

`00:53` If the equivalent amount of energy used to supply the USA with one day's electricity was used to power a car, it would be possible to drive round the world over 35,000 times.

`00:54` By the age of fifteen, 95 per cent of the population have developed some decay in their teeth.

`00:55` George III was terribly short-sighted.

`00:56` Julius Caesar always wore a laurel wreath to disguise his baldness.

`00:57` A newly born baby panda is smaller than a mouse.

`00:58` At birth our muscles are only one fortieth of their eventual power and size.

`00:59` Gorillas are vegetarians.

`01:00` If you smoke twenty cigarettes a day you inhale half a cup full of tar a year.

`01:01` During its first two and a half months' screening, the film 'Jaws' made five million pounds a week.

`01:02` Horses and zebras clean themselves by rolling in dust.

`01:03` The door to Number Ten Downing Street has to be opened from the inside; there is no key hole on the outside.

`01:04` Eighty per cent of the animals on earth are insects.

`01:05` The ant has a larger brain, for its size, than any other animal.

`01:06` The brain is made up of 9000 million cells.

`01:07` Blonde beards grow much more quickly than dark beards.

`01:08` In 1910 there was an outbreak of the plague in Sussex.

`01:09` In Scotland it is considered bad luck for a bride to try on her bridal gown before the wedding day.

`01:10` The chime of Big Ben can be heard ten miles away.

`01:11` In Madagascar the silk from spiders' webs is woven into cloth.

`01:12` The female Black Widow spider eats her husband after they have mated.

`01:13` There are twenty-two more miles of canal in Birmingham than in Venice.

`01:14` Her Majesty the Queen is forbidden to enter the House of Commons.

`01:15` Thrushes can sing fifty-five songs without ever repeating themselves.

`01:16` The word 'Amen' is Hebrew for 'So be it'.

`01:17` Mrs Alton Clapp talked non-stop for 96 hours 45 minutes and 1 second.

`01:18` Hans Lanseth, born in 1846, had a beard 5.4 metres long.

`01:19` The novelist Gustave Flaubert often spent one whole week writing a single word. It is also said that he would spend a morning putting a comma in, and the afternoon taking it out.

`01:20` King Richard I, better known as the 'Lion Heart', only spent six months of his ten-year reign in England.

`01:21` The Australian dog called a Dingo is the only animal inhabitant of that country to eat meat.

`01:22` The Romans introduced marbles to this country in the first century AD.

`01:23` Kay Price of Adelaide typed non-stop for 53 hours in 1962.

`01:24` 'Mohammed' is the most common first name in the world.

`01:25` London has only had seven white Christmases since 1900.

`01:26` Forty-two million people died as a result of the Black Death in the thirteenth century.

`01:27` The Vinegar River in Columbia contains so much acid that no fish can live there.

01:28 Aeschylus was killed when he was hit on the head by a tortoise, dropped from above by an eagle.

01:29 George Washington used to soak his false teeth in port to improve their flavour.

01:30 In Greece milk is often sold frozen on a stick to make it easier to carry.

01:31 Tin cans are over 90 per cent steel.

01:32 A hippopotamus can run faster than a man.

01:33 A newly hatched crocodile is three times larger than the egg from which it comes.

01:34 If a man could jump as high as a flea, relative to his body size, he would clear St Paul's Cathedral.

01:35 George Washington's dentist pioneered the first drill by using his mother's spinning wheel.

01:36 The Baltic is the least salty sea in the world.

01:37 A snail moves at a rate of 61 cms an hour.

01:38 Peanuts are used in the manufacture of dynamite.

01:39 In July 1971 an American hen laid an egg containing nine yolks.

01:40 George Grogniet of Belgium ate forty-four boiled eggs in thirty minutes.

01:41 At Queanbeyan, Australia, there is a thirty-one-man tandem.

01:42 The nail on our middle finger grows the fastest, the thumb nail is the slowest.

01:43 Strings of beads are still used as money by the Kayan tribe of Borneo.

01:44 A pumpkin grown in Colorado weighed 198 pounds.

01:45 Dogs wag their tails as a sign of welcome, cats as a sign of warning.

01:46 The silk of a spider's web is stronger than a steel thread of the same diameter.

01:47 A mole can dig a tunnel 68 metres long in one night.

01:48 An average pencil can write for 56 kilometres.

`01:49` A ship's hull collects 100 tonnes of barnacles every year.

`01:50` Mary Queen of Scots was a very skilful billiards player.

`01:51` Microfilming was in use as early as 1870.

`01:52` Ninety-six per cent of babies arrive at different times from those predicted by doctors.

`01:53` In Germany a black eye is called a 'blue eye'.

`01:54` There are no snakes found in Ireland.

`01:55` Louis XIV developed a stomach twice the size of an ordinary man's.

`01:56` Pure gold is so soft that it can be moulded by the hands.

`01:57` The playwright, Ben Jonson, was buried in a sitting position.

`01:58` The Doomsday Book, compiled in 1087, lists 5624 water mills in Britain.

`01:59` The role of Hamlet consists of 11,610 words.

02:00 About 120 barrels of oil can be made from the blubber of a large blue whale.

02:01 It is possible to boil water in a paper bag.

02:02 A full moon is nine times brighter than a half moon.

02:03 The first printing press in America was set up in 1640.

02:04 The longest recorded nose belonged to Thomas Wedders and was 7½ inches long.

02:05 Indian women of the San Blas tribe paint black lines on their noses to make them appear longer.

02:06 Ladies in the sixteenth and seventeenth centuries wore their wedding rings on their thumbs.

02:07 A horse in Australia, called Monty, lived to be fifty-two years old.

02:08 A snail can crawl over a razor blade without hurting itself.

02:09 The last Dodo died in 1681. The bird is now extinct.

02:10 The yoyo was originally used as a weapon.

02:11 One hundred and ten million bottles of Coca-Cola are drunk each day.

02:12 Oxburgh Hall in Norfolk has been owned by the same family for 490 years.

02:13 A French actor called Pierre Messie could make his hair stand on end at will.

02:14 The largest sundial in the world is the great pyramid of Cheops in Egypt.

02:15 If a drop of whisky is squirted on to a scorpion's back, it will sting itself to death.

02:16 Mushrooms can break through concrete.

02:17 A black cat is considered very unlucky in France.

02:18 Elephants are surprisingly good swimmers.

02:19 The USA had no national anthem until 1931.

02:20 More germs are passed on by shaking hands than by kissing.

02:21 The sun weighs 330,000 times as much as the earth.

02:22 Tulips originated in Turkey, and 'tulip' is the Turkish word for 'Turban'.

02:23 Modern telescopes allow us to look at galaxies 4000 million light years away.

02:24 There are more acres in Yorkshire than there are words in the Bible.

02:25 William III, George I, George II, George III and George IV, all died on Sundays.

02:26 In 1790 George Washington spent $200 in two months on ice-cream.

02:27 A 50,000-year-old spear was found buried at Clacton-on-Sea, Essex.

02:28 William Shakespeare spelt his surname eleven different ways.

02:29 'Buddha' means the 'enlightened one'.

02:30 In 1857 the Queen's rat-catcher earned more than the Poet Laureate.

`02:31` Cats cannot taste sweet foods.

`02:32` Goldfish turn white if left in a dark room for a long period of time.

`02:33` A person can move as many as seventy times in one night whilst asleep.

`02:34` There is no word in the English language that rhymes with 'oblige'.

`02:35` Moths cannot eat: they have neither mouths nor stomachs.

`02:36` Soldiers in ancient Greece went into battle naked from the waist down.

`02:37` Middle names were once illegal in England.

`02:38` Shark skin used to be used as sandpaper.

`02:39` 'Ham' and 'Sandwich' are actual place names in Kent.

`02:40` The annual coal production in Russia could supply London with enough electricity for 107 years.

`02:41` There is a town in Australia called 'Banana'.

`02:42` Cows' milk contains twice as much protein as human milk.

`02:43` 'Cha' is the Chinese word for tea.

`02:44` There are 20,000 particles in one cubic inch of fog.

`02:45` In March 1808, L. T. Halifax walked two miles an hour for 100 consecutive hours.

`02:46` A poet called Petrus Placentius wrote a poem called 'Pugna Porcorum' in which every verse began with the letter P.

`02:47` The first big pendulum clock was ordered almost 700 years ago by King Edward I, to be placed on Westminster tower.

`02:48` The German poet, Hans von Thummel, was buried in the heart of an oak tree.

`02:49` When the number 2,071,723 is multiplied by 5,363,222,357 the curious sum of 11,111,111,111,111,111 is produced.

`02:50` The wife of a Pomeranian farmer of Prussia gave birth to eleven children in sixteen months (1880-81). She had sextuplets and quintuplets.

02:51 Francis I, King of France in the sixteenth century, issued a decree making the wearing of whiskers punishable by death.

02:52 Chou Kung, who invented the compass, had a swivel wrist and could turn his hand in a complete circle.

02:53 There are approximately 40,000 direct descendants of Confucius living in China at the present time.

02:54 Wormwood is not a worm nor a wood. It is a plant.

02:55 Philip II of Spain (1527-1598) possessed the largest heart of any known man.

02:56 The earth is thought to be 5500 million years old.

02:57 The greatest volcanic eruption was at Krakatoa in 1883, which blasted a hole 1000 feet below sea level. The sound was heard 3000 miles away and tidal waves were caused as far as the English channel 11,000 miles away.

02:58 There were no aircraft carriers in World War I. The first was commissioned in 1922.

`02:59` The speed of a tornado may be up to fifty miles an hour.

`03:00` An igloo is so strong that a polar bear can crawl over it without breaking in.

`03:01` Diamond is the hardest substance known to man and can only be cut by another diamond.

`03:02` There are 4000 different varieties of palm tree.

`03:03` Man's body temperature is at its lowest at 4.00 am.

`03:04` A mole will die if it goes without food for any longer than twelve hours.

`03:05` Raccoons wash their food before eating it.

`03:06` A kangaroo can jump approximately ten to fifteen feet in one leap.

`03:07` Whales have fixed eyes which means they have to turn their whole bodies when they want to look in a different direction.

`03:08` An elephant's trunk is so sensitive at the tip that it is capable of picking up a small pin.

03:09 Dinosaurs became extinct approximately sixty million years ago.

03:10 A centipede can have as few as thirty legs.

03:11 Only the male nightingale sings, and it is pure fallacy that they only sing at night.

03:12 Starfish are capable of re-growing broken arms.

03:13 Oysters can live up to four months out of water.

03:14 In ancient Rome the average for a person to live was twenty-three years.

03:15 The human intestines are approximately thirty feet long.

03:16 Coffee can act as a poison when taken in very large doses.

03:17 According to legend, Adam and Eve ate the forbidden fruit on a Friday, which is why Friday the thirteenth is considered to be a very unlucky day.

03:18 The first comic strips appeared in England in 1900.

`03:19` Julius Caesar established the first newspaper in 60 BC. It was called 'Acta Diurna', which meant 'Daily Happenings'.

`03:20` The first opera was written in 1600. It was performed at the wedding of Henry IV of France.

`03:21` The Olympic Games are more than 2500 years old.

`03:22` Football as we know it was first played in 1869, although a similar game actually existed as far back as Roman and Spartan times.

`03:23` Ancient Egyptian mummies provide us with evidence that medical operations have been performed for thousands of years. For example, cataracts were removed from the eyes with thorns.

`03:24` It was not until about 100 years ago that people began to bath regularly.

`03:25` Chickens were known in China 3500 years ago.

`03:26` Four billion pounds of soap is manufactured annually in Britain.

`03:27` Wallpaper was used in Europe as long ago as 1481.

03:28 There is no rice in rice paper.

03:29 It is quite common for an elephant to live for a century.

03:30 In 1745 a watchmaker exhibited a flea tied by a chain of 200 links, with a padlock and key – the whole weighing only one third of a grain.

03:31 In 1833 a bed was manufactured in Paris that played music whenever anyone lay on it. It cost 780,000 francs.

03:32 The French horn is actually an English woodwind instrument.

03:33 If any whole number is decreased by the sum of its digits the remainder is always exactly divisible by nine.

03:34 The largest eggs are laid by sharks.

03:35 Japanese cherry trees bear no fruit; they are grown purely for ornamentation.

03:36 There is a stream in South America that flows both ways.

03:37 The Belgian hare is not a hare – it is a rabbit.

03:38 If the earth was composed of steel it would weigh 6,552,000,000,000,000,000,000

03:39 Earrings are considered to be a cure for sore eyes.

03:40 Francoise de Lorraine was married at the age of three to the four-year-old son of Henry IV of France.

03:41 A 14-inch cube of gold weighs one ton.

03:42 The fish known as the Beaked Chaetodon uses its nose as a gun and shoots drops of water at insects.

03:43 The name 'Jeep' originates from the letters GP which were stencilled on to this 'General Purpose' car.

03:44 No one has ever succeeded in arranging five cubes with six letters on each cube into every possible combination, because there are 620,448,401,735,259,439,369,000 possible combinations.

03:45 There is no soda in soda water.

03:46 Peter the Great became Czar of Russia at the age of ten.

03:47 In 1765 Walter Willey devoured a six-pound roast goose and a loaf of bread, and drank three quarts of port, without any ill effect.

03:48 Once a tiger has tasted human flesh it becomes a man-eater forever. One tiger in Nepal ate over 430 people.

03:49 Mustard stimulates egg production in chickens.

03:50 We have never seen more than one half of the moon because as it travels round the earth the same side is always facing us.

03:51 The Red Cross flag is the same as the flag of Switzerland but with the colours reversed.

03:52 Elephants sleep in a kneeling position.

03:53 Mary Queen of Scots had a watch shaped like a skull, measuring three inches in diameter.

03:54 Daniel McCurtley, of Kerry in Ireland, died in 1752 at the age of 111. When aged eighty he married his fifth wife, aged just fifteen, by whom he had no fewer than fifteen children.

03:55 In 1811 a blacksmith devoured two pints of winkles complete with shells in twenty minutes for a wager, and promptly died.

03:56 The first metal clock was invented in China in 263 BC.

03:57 If you freeze a bucket of salt water the ice will be free of salt.

03:58 In the Arctic a conversation can be heard two miles away.

03:59 Barn owls eat their prey whole and disgorge what they cannot digest.

04:00 Burning at the stake was a legal execution as late as 1800 in the USA.

04:01 You can spin only hard boiled eggs, not raw ones.

04:02 One very rare metal called gallium has such a low melting point, that if you hold a piece in your hand it will eventually melt.

04:03 Goldfish can survive being frozen to 310 degrees below zero.

04:04 The earth revolves around the sun at a speed eight times faster than that of a bullet from a gun.

`04:05` The fear of beds is known as 'clinophobia'.

`04:06` In July 1765 a cow gave birth to a calf that had two heads.

`04:07` Spaghetti originates from China.

`04:08` There is a city in the Sahara built entirely of salt.

`04:09` If you write a letter to nine different people, and the next day they each write a letter to nine people, and the process is continued for ten days, approximately 3500 million people would receive letters.

`04:10` The greyhound is the oldest known breed of dog.

`04:11` White bread was originally used only in church services.

`04:12` It would take 2,487,996 years to arrange fifteen books into every possible combination at the rate of one change per minute.

`04:13` In the seven years that William Wordsworth was Poet Laureate he did not publish one single line of new poetry.

04:14 Nelson suffered from severe sea sickness throughout his life.

04:15 Oil and water will mix – if you add detergent.

04:16 A hat worn by Napoleon fetched £1920 at an auction in London held in 1891.

04:17 It would take 3½ minutes to receive a radio message sent from Mars.

04:18 A pint of petrol has as much explosive power as a pound of dynamite.

04:19 In September 1886 a cricket match was played at Crystal Palace with both sides using broomsticks instead of bats.

04:20 A few drops of black paint added to a tin of white paint will make it even whiter.

04:21 In 1386 a pig was publicly hanged for killing a child.

04:22 In 1970 hailstones measuring 7½ inches in diameter fell in the US state of Kansas.

04:23 An ounce of gold could be beaten into enough gold leaf to cover an acre.

04:24 In 1820 a man took his wife to market and sold her for five shillings (twenty-five new pence).

04:25 Spiders spin their webs at night.

04:26 A cat's eyes appear to glow in the dark because they reflect the light.

04:27 The belief that drinking hot tea in hot weather cools you is false. Drinking hot tea may make you *feel* cooler, but it actually warms your body. If you want to cool down you should drink cold water.

04:28 The guillotine was first used on April 25th, 1792, for the execution of a highwayman. It was invented by Dr Guillotine as a means of avoiding unnecessary pain.

04:29 At night, clouds are lower than during the day.

04:30 Alfred Nobel, founder of the Nobel Peace Prize, invented dynamite, which has caused the deaths of millions of people.

04:31 It takes 120 drops of water to fill a teaspoon.

`04:32` Flamingos eat with their heads upside down.

`04:33` The Rock of Gibraltar is made of very soft limestone.

`04:34` A prairie dog is not a dog but a rodent.

`04:35` An egg can be made to stand on one end by shaking it so that the yolk is broken and settles at the bottom.

`04:36` The number 13 is considered lucky in Italy.

`04:37` Kern, the architect of St Basil's cathedral in Moscow, had his eyes put out by Ivan the Terrible in order to prevent him building a similar church elsewhere.

`04:38` Pure gold is so soft that one ounce could be drawn out to make a very thin wire 50 miles long.

`04:39` Ninety men on board Columbus's ship were prison convicts.

`04:40` Venus rotates clockwise; all other planets rotate anti-clockwise.

`04:41` In September 1944 an American lawyer left £25,000 to his cat.

04:42 A man pronounced dead in 1562 was buried. Six hours later his brother felt that he might be alive and the body was disinterred. The man was found to be alive and lived another seventy years, dying at the age of 105.

04:43 Giant bamboos in South East Asia can grow up to one metre in twenty-four hours.

04:44 A whale is not a fish, but a warm-blooded mammal.

04:45 Bombay Duck is made from fried fish and curry.

04:46 Richard Porson (1750 – 1808) was able to recite all of John Milton's *Paradise Lost* – backwards!

04:47 Over four fifths of all the greenery on earth is found in the world's oceans and seas.

04:48 The Great White Shark is the only creature living in the sea which has no natural enemies.

04:49 From the top of Mount Irazo in Costa Rica both the Pacific and Atlantic Oceans can be seen.

`04:50` Diamonds were more commonly worn by men than women until the fifteenth century.

`04:51` Cleopatra's Needle in London has no connection with Cleopatra. It is one of two which were erected in Egypt over 1000 years before she was born.

`04:52` Catgut comes from sheep, not cats.

`04:53` The Great Wall of China is eighteen feet thick and 1500 miles long.

`04:54` The elephant is the only animal that has been taught to stand on its head.

`04:55` Camel-hair brushes are made from squirrel hair.

`04:56` In 1348 it rained continually in England from June until Christmas.

`04:57` The soya bean has been eaten by the Chinese for 5000 years.

`04:58` The painter, Leonardo Da Vinci, could break a horse-shoe with his bare hands.

`04:59` Charles Dickens always wrote facing north.

05:00 The eyes of Chinese people are not slanted, it is only their eyelids that are almond-shaped.

05:01 The average person is estimated to walk 65,000 miles in a lifetime.

05:02 The Sphinx is the oldest statue in the world.

05:03 Miss Fanny Miles of Cincinnati had feet 60 cms long.

05:04 In 1650 the Oxford University anatomy department acquired the body of Anne Green, who had been hanged for murder. The deceased was found, however, to be still alive: she was revived and made a complete recovery.

05:05 Bears climb telegraph poles in the search for honey. The humming of the wires resembles that of bees.

05:06 A person can float in salt water, but swims better in fresh water.

05:07 Uranus takes 84 years to orbit the sun.

05:08 The tomato used to be considered poisonous.

05:09 The smallest church in the world is in Kentucky and has only three seats.

05:10 The substance that comes closest to the chemical construction of blood is seawater.

05:11 A baby was baptised as a girl in 1818, by mistake. It was re-baptised as a boy two weeks later.

05:12 The orange is one of the few fruits that will not ripen after plucking.

05:13 Cockroaches have remained on earth unchanged for 250 million years.

05:14 The ostrich only sticks its head in the sand to search for food or when covering its eggs for protection.

05:15 Surgeons in ancient Egypt had their hands cut off if their patients died.

05:16 A fly's eye has 4000 facets, which enable it to see an enemy approaching from any direction.

05:17 President Theodore Roosevelt gave his name to the Teddy Bear.

05:18 The largest shadow ever seen by man on earth is that made by the moon during an eclipse.

`05:19` Nearly half the population of the world lives in only one thirtieth of the total land area.

`05:20` The Hawaiian alphabet consists of only twelve letters.

`05:21` Jedediah Buxton went to see Garrick in 'Richard II', in the middle of the eighteenth century, and counted every word spoken by each actor.

`05:22` Beethoven composed most of his greatest music after he had become stone deaf.

`05:23` One fifth of the oxygen we inhale is used by the brain.

`05:24` Red rain fell on the coast of Newfoundland in 1890.

`05:25` In the time of Elizabeth I, men with beards had to pay a special tax.

`05:26` The Romans were the first to discover the use of arches.

`05:27` One third of the world's cattle population is in India. They are, however, never killed as they are considered sacred in India.

`05:28` Chewing gum while peeling onions prevents you from crying.

`05:29` Mourners in Persia used to have their tears bottled, as they were thought to be remedies for various illnesses.

`05:30` The sky is actually colourless. The colour is caused by the reflection of the sun's rays.

`05:31` Light from Pluto takes six years to reach Earth.

`05:32` There is no lead in a lead pencil: the core is made from graphite.

`05:33` Birds cannot fly in heavy fog.

`05:34` The left side of your brain controls the right side of your body.

`05:35` Horses show anger by laying back their ears.

`05:36` A female mosquito can produce 150 billion offspring.

`05:37` One sixth of the land on earth is in the Soviet Union.

`05:38` The turkey comes originally from North America.

05:39 In 1979 there was a snow storm over the Sahara Desert in southern Algeria.

05:40 The light of a firefly is so strong that it can shine through the stomach of a frog.

05:41 There are 1000 volcanoes on earth – only one third are active.

05:42 The humming-bird hums with its wings.

05:43 Overweight schoolchildren often eat less than their slimmer contemporaries.

05:44 The human eye is able to distinguish between two million colours and shades.

05:45 Elephants cannot jump.

05:46 The rainbow trout makes its nest from pebbles which it carries in its mouth.

05:47 President John F. Kennedy used to read four newspapers in twenty minutes.

05:48 In the history of the world there have been ten years of war to every year of peace.

05:49 Ants are capable of pulling weights three hundred times their own weight.

05:50 A cubic foot of warm water weighs less than a cubic foot of cold water.

05:51 The name 'Spain' is a Carthaginian word meaning 'Land of rabbits'.

05:52 In 1812 a Scottish clergyman undertook to read six chapters of the Bible every hour for 1000 consecutive hours. After thirteen days he fell into a profound sleep from which he never recovered.

05:53 Brushing your teeth with salt is as effective as using toothpaste.

05:54 Jupiter is large enough to contain all the other planets in the solar system.

05:55 In 1884 a patent was taken out in Germany for a 'Musical Cigar'.

05:56 The shortest will on record (1895): 'All to Mother.'

05:57 King Alfred was the first to mark candles into equal sections so that each section burned in a given time.

05:58 The actor Danny Kaye made his stage debut playing the role of a watermelon seed.

05:59 The nineteenth chapter of the second Book of Kings (Old Testament) and the thirty-seventh chapter of Isaiah (Old Testament) are exactly the same.

06:00 Weather vanes point in the opposite direction to which the wind is blowing.

06:01 There is a variety of orchid that has a pod which holds about seventy million seeds.

06:02 The increase in the world's population in just two years today is the same as the total population living at the time of Julius Caesar.

06:03 The only natural blue food is the bilberry.

06:04 At 25,000 feet a pilot can see for almost 194 miles.

06:05 In New York it is an offence to leave a shop-window dummy standing naked.

06:06 It is widely believed in France that if a bachelor steps on a cat's tail he will not find a wife for at least another year.

06:07 A lizard known as the 'Glass Snake' snaps into pieces as soon as you touch it.

06:08 Horses can fall asleep standing up.

06:09 The kiwi is the only bird to have nostrils at the end of its beak.

06:10 An epitaph in Bacton, Norfolk:

We	Must	All	Die
Must	We	Die	All
All	Die	We	Must
Die	All	Must	We

06:11 In Jamaica there are some oysters which live in trees.

06:12 The commonest name for a pub in Great Britain is the 'Red Lion'.

06:13 King William IV of Great Britain was also William I of Hanover, William II of Ireland, and William III of Scotland.

06:14 Windsor Castle is the largest inhabited castle in the world.

06:15 Buddhists all celebrate their birthday on New Year's Day.

06:16 Grasshoppers have white blood.

06:17 The perfume Eau De Cologne was originally produced as a means of protection against the plague.

06:18 In the Argentine the man in the moon appears upside down.

06:19 In Scott, Virginia, there is a railway tunnel which was originally carved by a river through 1557 feet of solid rock.

06:20 In 1592 the winter in Austria was so severe that wolves entered Vienna and attacked men and cattle.

06:21 The sun burns 240 million tons of hydrogen dust every minute.

06:22 At the age of ninety-four our hearts pump half the amount of blood they were pumping when we were twenty.

06:23 Henry VIII was a celebrated hammer-thrower as a young man.

06:24 In Trondheim, Norway, there is a village called 'Hell'.

06:25 In early Christian art the peacock was a symbol of resurrection.

06:26 In July 1812 an orphaned baby was suckled by a maltese goat on board a frigate named 'Swallow'.

`06:27` Twenty per cent of the Christmas cards bought today are sold in aid of charities.

`06:28` A sea urchin walks on the ends of its spines.

`06:29` The official national emblem of Wales is a daffodil, not a leek.

`06:30` A hearse in Connecticut had the sinister registration number U2.

`06:31` An epitaph in a churchyard at Newmarket:
> Here lies in silent clay
> Miss Arabella Young
> Who on the 21st of May
> Began to hold her tongue.

`06:32` In some parts of Britain, fried mice (fried alive) used to be regarded as a cure for smallpox.

`06:33` In Japan only the Imperial family are allowed to drive in a maroon-coloured car.

`06:34` Tin was the first metal ever to be used by man.

`06:35` The division of day and night into equal parts was invented about 4000 years ago.

06:36 Twenty-six countries in the world have no coastline at all.

06:37 If you are in a steel-roofed car you cannot be struck by lightning.

06:38 It is possible to see a rainbow as a complete circle from an aeroplane.

06:39 The cashew nut belongs to the poison ivy family.

06:40 Clams can live for 100 years.

06:41 In Rome gladiators' blood used to be drunk as a medicine.

06:42 A fish's heart has two chambers.

06:43 Mozart composed, rehearsed and first performed his *Linz* Symphony all in the space of five days.

06:44 The only animal that cries is man.

06:45 When an auctioneer named Knight died at Greenwood his epitaph ran:
Good Knight
Going
Going
Gone
1868

06:46 Tea used to be pronounced 'tay' in the seventeenth century.

06:47 There are more than twenty metals of more value than gold.

06:48 Rossini wrote 'The Barber of Seville' in eight days.

06:49 Henry Lewis, an English billiards player, could play with his nose instead of a cue.

06:50 In 1726 Charles Sanson, aged seven years, inherited the post of executioner.

06:51 The human mouth contains more bacteria than any other orifice in the body.

06:52 The only part of a reindeer worth eating is the tongue.

06:53 In Cuba there is a crocodile farm with 12,000 crocodiles.

06:54 In 1969 black snow fell in Sweden.

06:55 A frog has no neck and, therefore, cannot turn its head.

`06:56` A dog turns round before lying down to find which way the wind is blowing, and faces it to scent danger.

`06:57` A 65-year-old man has the same muscle power as a 25-year-old woman.

`06:58` A shark's skeleton has no bone, it is cartilage.

`06:59` The coldest place on earth is Verkhoyansk in Northern Siberia.

`07:00` It is possible to bore holes in solid material with a noise of 210 decibels.

`07:01` Shakespeare never saw an actress in his life; all the parts were played by men.

`07:02` The word 'and' appears in the Bible 46,227 times.

`07:03` A mature beech tree may give off as much as 680 litres of water on a warm day.

`07:04` A fully grown walrus yields seventy gallons of pure oil.

`07:05` Banana oil is not made from bananas. It is a by-product of petroleum.

07:06 The first astronauts in Skylab carried pills for travel sickness.

07:07 The hair spring of a watch was originally a pig's hair.

07:08 A ball of Black Widow spider webs no bigger than a pea would measure about thirty miles if all the threads were straightened out.

07:09 In France, AM is actually PM, for 'apres-midi' means afternoon'.

07:10 A brush used for varnishing will give 100 times as much wear as one used for painting.

07:11 Table-tennis used to be called 'Gossima'.

07:12 The third hand on a watch is in fact the second hand.

07:13 Benjamin Franklin invented the harmonica, the rocking-chair, the lightning-conductor, and double spectacles.

07:14 The game of chess originated in India 1500 years ago.

07:15 The Gaboon viper has fangs 50 mm long, the longest of any snake in the world.

07:16 Otters can slip into water without causing a splash.

07:17 An egg will float in a glass of water if you add sugar.

07:18 A typical plant only receives one tenth of its nutrition from the soil. The rest comes from the atmosphere.

07:19 There is a river called Aa in Pas de Calais, France.

07:20 It takes port forty years to reach ideal maturity.

07:21 The funny bone in our arm is a nerve.

07:22 A giraffe is the tallest animal in the world, but is incapable of uttering a sound.

07:23 Drumskins are made from the skin of an ass.

07:24 Radium is worth 24,000 times its weight in pure gold.

07:25 If three rays of light cross, red, yellow, and blue, they will produce a white light.

07:26 The only apostle to die a natural death was St John the Evangelist.

07:27 If a person in Australia could shout loudly enough to be heard in New York, the sound would take fourteen hours to reach there.

07:28 The camel has no gall bladder.

07:29 Over twice as many American psychologists commit suicide each year as their mental patients.

07:30 There is a lake in Haute Garonne, France, called 'Co'.

07:31 The giraffe can live longer in a desert without water than a camel, and is capable of running faster than a horse.

07:32 Eskimos have refrigerators to *stop* their meat from freezing.

07:33 Until 1957 London was the largest city in the world.

07:34 The sailfish can swim faster than a horse can gallop.

`07:35` In 1927 Miss Joyce Wethered, the British champion woman golfer, hit a swallow with a golf ball.

`07:36` In 1806 a partridge was shot and was found to have two necks branching from the body.

`07:37` In 1940 a bird's nest was discovered that had been built entirely of confetti.

`07:38` Henry Ford once tried to buy the Eiffel Tower and take it to America.

`07:39` Buddhist burials take a long time because gravediggers have to be very careful when digging not to harm a worm.

`07:40` The first thermometers were so large that they took five minutes to tell a person's body temperature.

`07:41` St Patrick, patron saint of Ireland, was a Frenchman.

`07:42` In 1670 a plague of fleas in Munster, Germany, was found guilty of disorderly conduct and was banished for ten years.

`07:43` The poison cyanide can be producd from plum stones and apple pips.

07:44 Bees die immediately they have stung.

07:45 A sparrow's brain is far larger in proportion to its body size than that of a man.

07:46 In 1925 it was so cold that the Niagara Falls froze.

07:47 After she lost all her teeth, Elizabeth I used to stuff her mouth with cloth whenever she appeared in public. She did this to stop her face from looking sunken and hollow.

07:48 Peter Arbuez, known as the Grand Inquisitor, burned no fewer than 40,000 people at the stake, and was made a saint by the Pope in 1860.

07:49 A Queen ant can lay up to sixty eggs a minute, and lives for several years.

07:50 Cyrus, King of Persia in the fifth century BC, was said to know the names of all the soldiers in his army.

07:51 Great Dane dogs come from Germany and have nothing to do with Denmark.

07:52 The two longest words in the Bible are 'Commandments' and 'Testimonies'.

07:53 Cows can be identified by their nose-prints in the same way that we can be identified by our fingerprints.

07:54 We have enough potassium in our bodies to explode a toy cannon.

07:55 In chess there are 197,299 different ways of playing the first four moves.

07:56 A waterfall near Honolulu falls upwards, because of winds which catch the water and blow it back over a cliff.

07:57 On 9th June 1938, two Cambridge undergraduates walked backwards from Cambridge to Newmarket, a distance of 13 miles, in 5½ hours.

07:58 The bloodhound is so called because it is a 'blooded' or pure-bred dog.

07:59 In 1788, David Davis of Clapham left five shillings (twenty-five new pence) to Mary David, which was sufficient 'to enable her to get drunk for the last time at my expense'.

08:00 An Austrian woman burnt all her money before she died in 1917 because her relatives had been unkind to her pet cats.

08:01 An epitaph on a tombstone in Kirkeel (Yorkshire) churchyard:
Here lie the remains of Thomas Nicolls,
Who died in Philadelphia, March 1578.
Had he lived, he would have been buried here.

08:02 The chamois is able to stand on an area the size of a ten-pence piece.

08:03 The dormouse spends six months of the year in hibernation.

08:04 Ferrets catch colds in exactly the same way that we do.

08:05 Every tenth egg is larger than the preceeding nine.

08:06 Within two hours of standing in daylight a bottle of milk can lose up to two thirds of its vitamin B content.

08:07 Crocuses have been known to force their way through tarmac.

08:08 Imitation diamonds can be told from real ones, because real diamonds are always cold.

08:09 Cubes of ice wrapped in insulating glass fibre can be baked in an oven without melting.

08:10 The number of different kinds of insects alive today is greater than the total number of all the types of all the other animals added together.

08:11 The first atom bomb was equivalent to 20,000 tons of TNT, yet was contained in a tube measuring only three inches.

08:12 The Weihenstephen Brewery in Bavaria has been brewing beer for 900 years.

08:13 There is a butterfly found in Brazil that has the smell and colour of chocolate.

08:14 Our Queen Elizabeth II is the only monarch to have been born in a private house.

08:15 To test whether a metal is pure gold, apply nitric acid. Gold will remain unaffected, any other metal will turn green.

08:16 There is no such thing as one dice. The singular form of dice is 'die'.

08:17 The opposite sides of a die always add up to seven.

08:18 The hairs of a man's beard are as strong as copper wires of the same dimension.

08:19 British barristers still wear black, in mourning for Queen Anne who died in 1694.

08:20 A raisin dropped in a glass of champagne will move up and down continuously.

08:21 Indian ink actually comes from China.

08:22 The frog's tongue grows from the front of its mouth.

08:23 There are at least eighty different varieties of rice grown in India.

08:24 It is considered unwise to eat oysters in a month without an R in it.

08:25 A method of execution in Mongolia was to nail the condemned into a box and leave him.

08:26 A law in the fourteenth century made it illegal for a man to eat more than two meals a day.

08:27 In the USA somebody dies of cancer every ninety seconds.

08:28 The clock in Salisbury cathedral has no face. The time can only be told by its chimes.

08:29 A thick glass is more likely to crack if it has hot water poured into it than a thin glass.

08:30 The poet Byron kept a bear as a pet.

08:31 In 1696 a two-storey church was built inside an oak tree in France.

08:32 In Hampshire there is a place called Middle Wallop and one called Nether Wallop. Wallop means a river valley.

08:33 A knitting machine was invented in 1589.

08:34 A safety-pin was invented in Greece in the eighth century BC.

08:35 When a piece of glass cracks the cracks move at 4800 kilometres per hour.

08:36 Walking fast uses eight times as many calories as writing.

08:37 A ten-gallon hat holds only six pints.

08:38 The word 'onion' comes from the Latin 'unio', which means 'large pearl'.

08:39 The snail's teeth are arranged in rows along the edge of its tongue.

08:40 The 'Mona Lisa' was first bought by King Francis I of France to decorate his bathroom.

08:41 Oaks and poplars are struck by lightning more frequently than other trees.

08:42 Hindu babies do not have their nails cut until they are one year old.

08:43 Holly leaves on a tree grow less prickly the higher up the tree they are.

08:44 Man can fly to the moon today in less time than it used to take to travel from one end of England to the other by stagecoach.

08:45 Over two tons of rock have to be mined in South Africa to extract less than one ounce of gold.

08:46 There is a town called 'A' in Sweden.

08:47 The seahorse is able to grasp objects with its tail.

08:48 Pontius Pilate is considered a saint in the Ethiopian Church.

08:49 A sneeze can travel as fast as 100 miles an hour.

`08:50` In its normal state natural gas has no smell.

`08:51` An English sentence which contains all the letters of the alphabet: 'The quick brown fox jumps over the lazy dog'.

`08:52` The seventeenth King of Poland, John III, was born, crowned and married on 17th June, and ironically died on 17th June too.

`08:53` American Indians used to smoke through their noses.

`08:54` The Red Sea is never mentioned by name in the Bible.

`08:55` A man normally breathes about six and a half quarts of air every minute.

`08:56` It takes forty-three muscles to frown, but only seventeen to smile.

`08:57` Dentists extract four tons of rotting teeth every year from children.

`08:58` Blind people who have been blind from birth only dream sounds.

`08:59` If you ran at a steady six miles an hour, it would take 173 days to run round the world.

09:00 It was believed in the past that kings should die standing up.

09:01 There are nearly 1000 different words for 'camel' in Arabic.

09:02 In a 72-year life-span the average human heart beats more than 3000 million times.

09:03 Early golf balls used to be made from leather bags stuffed with feathers.

09:04 A caterpillar has approximately 2000 muscles.

09:05 St Luke was the only New Testament writer who was not Jewish.

09:06 Snakes smell with their tongues.

09:07 Napoleon designed the Italian flag.

09:08 The windows of an empty house never frost over, however cold.

09:09 A dwarf called Geoffrey Hudson once fought a duel against a man twice his height and won.

09:10 A church in Toronto, Canada, is called the St James Bond United Church.

09:11 'Porridge' was originally a thick vegetable soup.

09:12 King George I of England could not speak one word of English.

09:13 A porcupine has 36,000 quills.

09:14 The Canadian river flows nowhere near Canada. It rises in the US state of Colorado and flows into the Arkansas River in Oklahoma.

09:15 No point in Britain is more than 120 kilometres from the sea.

09:16 Crickets hear through their knees.

09:17 Stamp collecting is the world's most popular hobby.

09:18 The redwood tree has a fireproof bark.

09:19 The human neck has the same number of vertebrae as a giraffe's.

09:20 The late John Wayne was christened Marion Morrison.

09:21 Birds are sometimes able to set their own broken wings.

09:22 In *Gulliver's Travels* Jonathan Swift described the two moons of Mars, 150 years before either moon was discovered.

09:23 The distance between the earth and the sun is approximately 385 times the distance between the earth and the moon.

09:24 Lettuce is the most widely eaten green vegetable in the world.

09:25 One tonne of uranium produces the same amount of energy as 30,000 tonnes of coal.

09:26 An ice cube in a glass of water will not raise the water level when it melts.

09:27 Saudi Arabia imports sand from Scotland and camels from North Africa.

09:28 An elephant's height can be calculated by measuring the distance around its foot and doubling it.

09:29 The Romans were very fond of eating dormice.

09:30 Some locusts spend fifteen years as grubs and then only live for a matter of weeks as adults.

`09:31` It takes more calories to eat a piece of celery than celery has in it in the first place.

`09:32` If a person started counting at the moment of birth and continued until he was sixty-five, he still would not have counted as far as a thousand million.

`09:33` Milk is heavier than cream.

`09:34` If you touch the leaves of the sensitive plant they will move away from you.

`09:35` The number 37 cannot be divided by any other number.

`09:36` In the Great Fire of London in 1666 there were only six deaths.

`09:37` A jumbo jet weighs as much as sixty-seven African elephants.

`09:38` The average person consumes about one ton of food and drink a year.

`09:39` A sharp cough may move air inside your body faster than the speed of sound.

`09:40` A prison on the Isle of Sark holds two prisoners.

`09:41` Charles Dickens, author of *Oliver Twist*, had a childhood friend called Bob Fagin.

`09:42` The human brain is incapable of feeling pain.

`09:43` During the last 130 years, fifteen buildings have been hit by meteorites.

`09:44` In the Caribbean Bahamas there are 3000 islands, only twenty of which are inhabited.

`09:45` Sir Arthur Conan Doyle, the author of *Sherlock Holmes*, was a doctor by profession.

`09:46` The funeral procession of a Chinese General lasted for a year.

`09:47` The Matani Tribe of West Africa used to play football with a human skull.

`09:48` St John's Lane in Rome is just 48 cms wide.

`09:49` The place where children go in *Peter Pan* is wrongly called 'Never-Never Land'; the author in fact called it 'Neverland'.

`09:50` Ducks only lay eggs in the morning.

09:51 The bat is the only mammal that can fly.

09:52 One hundred and eighty medical journals are published every hour around the world.

09:53 Poodles do not shed their hair.

09:54 A law in Ohio, USA, requires all domestic animals to wear a light when they go out at night.

09:55 An owl cannot see in total darkness.

09:56 The only insect to produce a food eaten by man is the bee.

09:57 A whip cracks because its tip moves faster than the speed of sound.

09:58 In the thirteenth century eggs were two pence for one hundred.

09:59 In Iraq you can eat snakes any day of the week except Sunday.

10:00 An owl's eye occupies one sixth of its head.

10:01 Humans blink twenty-five times each minute.

`10:02` An emu can run up to thirty miles per hour.

`10:03` The starfish is capable of turning its stomach inside out.

`10:04` Pepsi-Cola was first introduced as a cure for hangovers.

`10:05` Passenger coaches were using sprung suspension in 1580.

`10:06` Jane Austen, Joan of Arc and Florence Nightingale never married.

`10:07` Brussel sprouts lose 90 per cent of their vitamin C content in cooking.

`10:08` In 1971 the world's poorest people were found in the Philippines – they had no clothes, no farming, and lived without the wheel or pottery.

`10:09` Human eyes are so sensitive that on a clear moonlit night a person on a mountain peak could see a match struck fifty miles away.

`10:10` There is only one lake in Scotland, the rest are lochs.

`10:11` Two people have thrown an egg to each other a distance of 98 metres without it breaking.

`10:12` The wettest place in the world is a mountain in Hawaii with 932 cm of rain a year.

`10:13` In 1969 Paul Tully of Brisbane ate thirty bags of crisps in 24 minutes and 33 seconds.

`10:14` June Clark, aged seventeen, sneezed for 155 days in 1966.

`10:15` Bells were originally tolled at funerals to frighten off evil spirits.

`10:16` Tomatoes were originally called 'Love Apples'.

`10:17` In 1740 a cow was found guilty of witchcraft and hung on the gallows.

`10:18` Gunpowder was first used by British forces in 1346.

`10:19` Until 1789 lions were used to guard the Tower of London.

`10:20` Moslems always make a mistake when they make a Persian carpet as they consider that only Allah can make things perfectly.

`10:21` Between them, Americans carry an estimated two million tonnes of excess fat on their bodies.

`10:22` Millions of meteorites crash into the earth's atmosphere every day. But nearly all of them are burned up by friction before they reach the surface.

`10:23` A kiwi's beak is so sensitive it can detect worms in the ground.

`10:24` Most mammals cannot detect any colour and see things only in black and white.

`10:25` Taiwan is the largest exporter of mushrooms in the world.

`10:26` A cod's liver contains vitamins absorbed from the sun.

`10:27` The broad bean is the oldest vegetable known to man.

`10:28` A mass of iron weighing 40,000 tonnes fell in Siberia in 1908.

`10:29` The population of the world is growing at a rate of one and a half million every week.

`10:30` Whale meat is very rich in vitamin C.

`10:31` Dandelions contain a vast quantity of vitamin A.

10:32 Wire wool burns faster than sheep's wool.

10:33 In Central America there is a fish that has four eyes.

10:34 A town in Argentina is called 'Sauce'.

10:35 In 1800 portable showers were used in Paris for travellers.

10:36 People used to believe that cucumbers gave you cholera.

10:37 The word 'redivider' is the longest palindrome, that is it can be read backwards as well as forwards.

10:38 Seventy-five per cent more plants grow under the ocean than on land.

10:39 Crows can distinguish a man with a gun from one without.

10:40 The first TV cooking demonstration showed how to make an omelette.

10:41 We shed one complete outer layer of skin every four weeks.

10:42 In Turkey it is considered very bad luck to step on a piece of bread lying on the ground.

10:43 Arabic was not generally spoken in Egypt until the seventeenth century.

10:44 An electric eel can produce a shock of 400 volts.

10:45 In 1945 Big Ben was slowed down by five minutes when some starlings took a rest on the minute hand.

10:46 In the village of Troo, in France, there is a speaking well.

10:47 In the 1880s it was possible to buy two dozen live frogs for two shillings (ten new pence),

10:48 Abbad el Motaddid of Seville used the skulls of his enemies as flower pots.

10:49 In the Middle Ages nearly one day in three was a religious holiday.

10:50 'Evil' spelt backwards gives the word 'live'.

10:51 A camel's hump is fat.

10:52 The Chinese were the first to produce porcelain.

10:53 Ten thousand-year-old Lupin seeds have been successfully germinated.

`10:54` A four-month-old kitten once climbed to the top of the Matterhorn, 4503 metres.

`10:55` A Frenchman once built a clock out of old bicycles.

`10:56` The first piped water supply in England was installed in 1233.

`10:57` Christianity has more followers than any other religion on earth.

`10:58` The famous actress Sarah Bernhardt had a wooden leg in later life.

`10:59` Astronauts orbiting earth can sometimes see as many as sixteen sunrises and sunsets every twenty-four hours.

`11:00` It takes forty minutes to boil an ostrich egg.

`11:01` The Sequeru cactus grows branches that are sixteen times taller than a man.

`11:02` The diet of a normal American would kill a monkey in a very short time.

`11:03` The façade of the famous Paris art gallery, the Louvre, is 2½ miles long.

11:04	There is no mention in the Bible of Jonah being swallowed by a whale.
11:05	Spiritualist Amy MacPherson was buried with a live telephone in her coffin.
11:06	Touching wood for luck was an early Christian practice, for wood is symbolic of the cross.
11:07	Studies show that men are more likely to fall out of bed than women.
11:08	The name 'Sierra Leone' means 'Lion Mountain'.
11:09	Horses do not have collar bones.
11:10	Little Miss Muffet was a real person.
11:11	The Carpenter Frog has a croak that sounds like a blow from a hammer.
11:12	Crocodiles have semi-transparent eyelids.
11:13	Zebras' stripes are always different, like our fingerprints.
11:14	Hearts beat about seventy times a minute.

11:15 The first thimble was used only 300 years ago.

11:16 Only two angels are mentioned by name in the Bible. They are Michael and Gabriel.

11:17 In the Dominican Republic a divorce can be obtained in one day.

11:18 During the First World War parrots were kept in the Eiffel Tower, in Paris, to give warning of air-raids. Their hearing was so acute that they could hear approaching aircraft long before they were seen.

11:19 The Cambodian alphabet has seventy-two letters.

11:20 An opera singer was singing Benjamin Britten's 'Look where you go', when she accidentally stepped off the stage and fell into the orchestra pit.

11:21 The wearer of the first top hat was fined fifty pounds.

11:22 Girls tend to sleep more soundly than boys.

11:23 Over ten million people will have the same birthday as you.

11:24 The first and last letters of all the continents' names are alike.

11:25 Many insects, such as locusts, grasshoppers and ants, are eaten around the world.

11:26 The world's deepest mine is 3840 metres deep.

11:27 Leather has enough nutritional value to keep a human alive for a short time.

11:28 In Chinese writing the word 'malice' depicts three women.

11:29 Louis XIII of France was bled forty-seven times in one month.

11:30 A snake in London zoo was once fitted with an artificial eye.

11:31 There is no evidence to prove that Richard III had a hunchback.

11:32 The Century plant blooms every seven years.

11:33 A grasshopper's legs can walk on their own, even when detached from the body.

`11:34` A 'googol' is 10 to the power of 100. That is 1 with one hundred noughts after it.

`11:35` A music teacher in Paris named his children Do, Re, Mi, Fa. Sol, La, and Ti. The eighth child was named 'Octave'.

`11:36` Newspapers were once made out of rubber for people who read in the bath.

`11:37` Alcohol reduces the body's temperature.

`11:38` A method of suicide in China used to be to eat half a kilo of salt.

`11:39` Peacock feathers are considered to be very unlucky in the theatre.

`11:40` King John of France reigned for four days.

`11:41` King George V had the right to wear more than 100 military and naval uniforms.

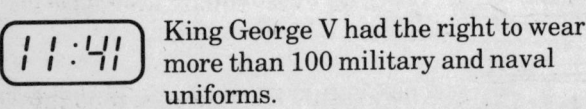 The Roman poet Virgil once spent £50,000 on the funeral of a pet fly.

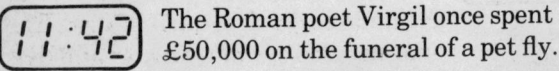 In 1922 a sixty-four-year-old woman pleaded guilty to sixty-one bigamous marriages that she had made in five years.

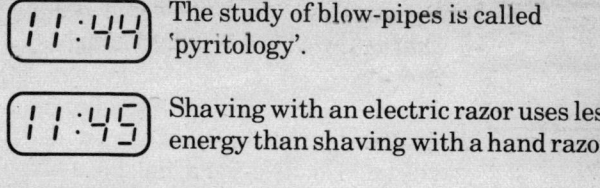

11:44 The study of blow-pipes is called 'pyritology'.

11:45 Shaving with an electric razor uses less energy than shaving with a hand razor.

11:46 When a lady's health was toasted in Rome it was the custom to have one glass of wine for every letter of her name.

11:47 One blue whale weighs as much as 480 lions, or 600 giraffes, or 120,000 hedgehogs, or 4,800,000 mice.

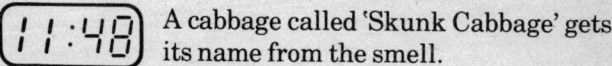

11:48 A cabbage called 'Skunk Cabbage' gets its name from the smell.

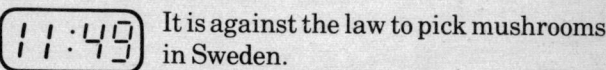

11:49 It is against the law to pick mushrooms in Sweden.

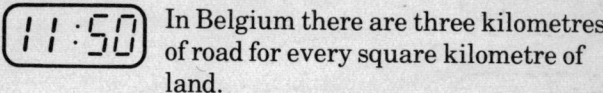

11:50 In Belgium there are three kilometres of road for every square kilometre of land.

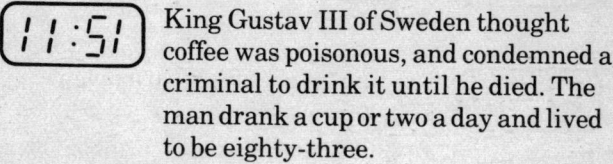

11:51 King Gustav III of Sweden thought coffee was poisonous, and condemned a criminal to drink it until he died. The man drank a cup or two a day and lived to be eighty-three.

11:52 'Dry ice' does not melt, it evaporates.

11:53 In 1904 12,400,000 razor blades were sold world-wide.

11:54 The Battle of Hastings was fought six miles from Hastings.

11:55 A reward of £30,000 was offered for the arrest of Bonny Prince Charlie.

11:56 The earth's crust is the same thickness in proportion to the earth as an eggshell is to an egg.

11:57 The earliest jeans cost seven pounds for a dozen pairs.

11:58 Monarch butterflies migrate more than 3,000 kilometres each year.

11:59 It takes 26,000 waking hours for anyone to learn to speak English as well as a six-year-old.

12:00 Lobsters live longer in sealed containers than in ones with air vents.

12:01 A giant water lily that grows in the Amazon is able to support a child.

12:02 In China a soup is made from real birds' nests.

12:03 India makes more films in a year than any other country.

12:04 The only miracle that appears in all four gospels of the New Testament is the feeding of the five thousand.

12:05 During the First World War troops smoked beech leaves to conserve tobacco.

12:06 In her novel *Northanger Abbey*, Jane Austen refers to baseball.

12:07 Seventeenth-century law in Massachusetts made it an offence to celebrate Christmas.

12:08 In Germany there is a breed of flea that lives in beer mats.

12:09 The ancient Egyptians believed that the world was hatched from an egg.

12:10 There are 3000 different languages in the world.

12:11 Shakespeare was the first to use the words 'dwindle' and 'hurry'.

12:12 Until the last century, solid blocks of tea were used as money in Siberia.

12:13 More than 100 million comets revolve around the sun.

`12:14` The Egyptians kept dachshunds over 4000 years ago.

`12:15` In Tibet it is a sign of respect to stick your tongue out at your guests.

`12:16` The murder rate in Medieval England was twenty-six times greater than it is today.

`12:17` In 1896 there was a war between Britain and Zanzibar which lasted 38 minutes.

`12:18` Glaciers cover 10 per cent of the earth's surface.

`12:19` Any five-digit number multiplied by 11 and then multiplied by 9091, will reappear twice in the product.

`12:20` President Carter saw a UFO during 1969.

`12:21` A cicada takes seventeen years to develop as a larva, but only lives for one month as an adult.

`12:22` There is a woman alive today whose great-uncle was alive in 1787.

`12:23` The French author, Stendhal, became a famous literary figure after he had been dead for 100 years.

12:24 In 1970 Robert Gardner of Stroud threw a brick 42.26 metres.

12:25 In America there is a woman whose name is 'Merry Christmas'.

12:26 A nanosecond is one thousandth of a millionth of a second.

12:27 'Odontophobia' is a fear of teeth.

12:28 Ice and concrete have a similar degree of hardness.

12:29 At the outbreak of the First World War the American Air Force consisted of fifty men.

12:30 It was against the law to play the drums in the Middle Eastern state of Oman until 1970.

12:31 To count to one billion (counting to 200 in one minute) it would take a person 19,024 years, 68 days, 10 hours and 40 minutes.

12:32 One bucketful of sea water contains about two cups of minerals.

12:33 Strips of steel are stronger than one solid piece.

12:34 The Icelandic capital Reykjavik is heated by hot water pumped from underground springs.

12:35 Boils can be cured by acupuncture.

12:36 We can distinguish between 10,000 different smells.

12:37 The last name in the San Francisco telephone directory is 'Zachry Zzzzra'.

12:38 On some parts of Mars the daily temperature range can be as much as 270°F.

12:39 The humming-bird cannot walk like other birds, and uses its feet only for perching.

12:40 Less than ten species have the teeth or jaws to eat man.

12:41 The colour combination with the strongest visual impact is black on yellow.

12:42 St Simeon the Younger spent the last forty-five years of his life sitting on a pole.

12:43 The Mimosa plant folds its leaves at night and appears to be asleep.

12:44 A dozen fireflies provide enough light to read by.

12:45 Up until 1905, criminals in China used to be branded with a hot iron.

12:46 There are almost three times as many species of plants as there are of animals.

12:47 In 1809 a celebrated walker walked 1000 miles in 1000 hours.

12:48 According to weather records kept over twenty years, Thursday has proved to be the wettest day of the week.

12:49 Fingerprints as a means of identification were first used 120 years ago.

12:50 In 1940 a circus performer was fired 53 metres from a cannon.

12:51 A sixteenth-century Chinese calendar was found engraved on the shoulder blade of an ox.

12:52 In the Atacama Desert it rained in 1971 for the first time in 400 years.

12:53 In the Philippines the Boya Bird builds fireflies into its nest which make it glow in the dark.

`12:54` The North Pole is 2799 metres lower than the South Pole.

`12:55` During an investigation inside a toad's stomach 363 ants were found.

`12:56` If a glass of water were magnified to the size of the earth, the water molecules would appear the size of oranges.

`12:57` In Berlin in 1900 a census showed that 240 women had between thirteen and twenty children.

`12:58` Seven and a half million tonnes of water evaporate from the Dead Sea every year.

`12:59` Lake Saikal, in Siberia, is so deep that it even has deep-sea fish.

`13:00` At any one minute there are 2000 thunder storms somewhere in the world.

`13:01` Palm trees in the Seychelle Islands grow coconuts weighing eighteen kilos.

`13:02` Denim was originally made in Nimes in France and called 'De Nimes'.

`13:03` A pythoness is a witch, not a snake.

13:04 You have a one in four million chance of being struck by lightning.

13:05 The tallest house of cards was made of 1240 playing cards.

13:06 An earthworm can pull ten times its own weight.

13:07 The total area of Japan is 147,000 square miles.

13:08 In Denmark it is common for women to smoke cigars.

13:09 When you get out of a bath you are covered with a film of water 0.5 mm thick.

13:10 The backbone of a camel is *perfectly* straight.

13:11 Baby seals are called 'pups'.

13:12 On the Island of Java there is a lake that blows bubbles.

13:13 Women had to cover their ears in the Middle Ages.

13:14 George IV was created the Earl of Chester when he was one week old.

`13:15` The ring-tailed lemur makes a miaow like a cat.

`13:16` It takes an English swallow just one month to migrate to Africa.

`13:17` A spider can lay 600 eggs at one time.

`13:18` The Marquis de Pelier was imprisoned for fifty years for whistling at Marie Antoinette.

`13:19` One man weighs the equivalent of 5000 mice.

`13:20` Brick walls and glass window panes are made from the same material – sand.

`13:21` In Norfolk there are two villages called 'Great Snoring' and 'Little Snoring'.

`13:22` Water is scarce in Morocco.

`13:23` The people of Iceland read more books per person than any other nation on earth.

`13:24` The Hurricane plant has holes in its leaves to protect it from being blown over by the wind.

13:25 Six thousand five hundred tons of hair-powder were used annually by the British army during the reign of George III.

13:26 In the eighteenth century ladies wore face patches to aid their beauty.

13:27 Rainbows only occur when the sun is at an angle of less than 40 degrees above the horizon.

13:28 Kangaroo means 'I don't know' – it is three Aborigine words 'Kan, ga, roo'.

13:29 Oliver Cromwell's surname was really 'Williams'.

13:30 The temperature inside the sun is thirty million degrees fahrenheit.

13:31 The first helicopter model was made by Leonardo da Vinci.

13:32 Jonathan Swift, author of *Gulliver's Travels*, refused to speak to anyone for a whole year.

13:33 The mangrove tree will grow in salt water.

13:34 If the roots of a pumpkin plant were streched out they would measure 24 kilometres.

13:35 The female starfish produces 200 million eggs every year.

13:36 A frog can jump twelve times its own length.

13:37 The humming-bird can fly backwards.

13:38 A kangaroo cannot jump with its tail off the ground.

13:39 The giant squid has eyes 275 mm across.

13:40 The human body has enough fat to make seven bars of soap.

13:41 A Danish linguist was able to speak 235 different languages.

13:42 The jaguar catches fish with its paws.

13:43 Medieval Japanese women used to paint their teeth black as a sign of beauty.

13:44 The telephone developed from experiments to produce a hearing aid.

13:45 St Nicholas is the patron saint of thieves.

13:46 The brain is four-fifths water.

13:47 Many breeds of tropical fish could survive in a tank of human blood.

13:48 In Kenya elephants bathe in pink mud which dries on them - hence, pink elephants.

13:49 Even though Europe is the second smallest continent in area, it has the second longest continental coastline.

13:50 There are about 500 different shades of grey between black and white.

13:51 The long-tailed fowl of Japan has a twenty-foot-long tail.

13:52 In 1970 Roger Martinez swallowed 225 live goldfish.

13:53 In 1326 you could buy a pair of glasses for two shillings (ten new pence).

13:54 Fire in cotton can be extinguished more effectively by petrol than water.

13:55 The Royal Mint only produced four pennies in 1933.

13:56 Russia uses more perfume than any other country in the world.

13:57 In Siberia being pelted by lice and slugs means 'I love you'.

13:58 A 40,000-year-old skull shows that man has always suffered from tooth decay.

13:59 A methodist preacher in his seventy-two-year life read the Bible from cover to cover 2600 times.

14:00 Lawn tennis was first played in 1879.

14:01 The Great Red Spot on the planet Jupiter is 25,000 miles wide.

14:02 Crushed strawberries can relieve sunburn.

14:03 Until less than one hundred years ago, corpses waiting to be buried were kept in the cellars of public houses.

14:04 Eating the bark of the pomegranate tree is supposed to cure tapeworms.

14:05 Piano keys are generally made from the wood of the horn beam.

14:06 In medieval England if you were engaged to someone and wanted to end the engagement you sent them a sprig of lilac.

14:07 Abraham Lincoln was the first President of the United States to be assassinated.

14:08 In 1972 a cat fell 49 metres from a building and survived.

14:09 A single drop of water contains 100 billion atoms.

14:10 A group of apes is called a 'shrewdness' of apes.

14:11 Christian Heinrich of Lübeck was able to talk when he was eight weeks old.

14:12 A pottle is a bottle containing two quarts.

14:13 Butterflies taste with their back legs.

14:14 When we blink, our eyelids close for one fifth of a second.

14:15 The tuna fish belongs to the mackerel family.

14:16 Mozart began composing music at the age of four.

14:17 Baked beans were introduced in 1830, but were served with molasses.

14:18 Dogs sweat through their paws.

14:19 In Britain at least one person in ten plays darts.

14:20 A station platform in Bengal is 833 metres long.

14:21 Prince Charles became Duke of Cornwall at the age of three.

14:22 Enid Blyton wrote a total of 600 children's stories.

14:23 In 1360 more knights were killed by lightning than were killed in battles.

14:24 At the present rate of erosion, the Niagara Falls will disappear in under 25,000 years.

14:25 During the winter of 1890-91 the Thames became completely frozen from Teddington to Lechlade.

14:26 Bees and rabbits come originally from Australia.

14:27 A mouse is so light that it could fall 1000 yards down a mine-shaft and not be killed.

14:28 The male Midwife Toad carries the eggs that its wife lays.

14:29 Salt was once so precious that explorers set out to look for it.

14:30 The village of Kempton, near Bradford, is a single street seven miles long.

14:31 It is impossible to make colourless wine.

14:32 On 2nd September 1752 the calendar was changed and jumped straight to the 14th September. The days in between, therefore, never existed.

14:33 Viscountess Astor was the first lady to take her seat in the House of Commons.

14:34 Only the male canary sings.

14:35 We spend one third of our lives asleep.

14:36 A 'fillip' is the name given to snapping your fingers together.

14:37 In 1972 the Royal Navy commissioned their first plastic warship.

14:38 An Indian poem called 'Mahabharata' contains nearly three million words.

14:39 The word 'Lord' appears 1855 times in the Bible.

14:40 Cleopatra was Greek.

14:41 The last Russian tsar, Nicholas II, seriously considered the idea of constructing an electric fence all round Russia.

14:42 The insulation in the fuel tanks of rockets is so effective that it would take an ice cube eight years to melt.

14:43 In ancient Greece camel meat was considered a delicacy.

14:44 A cat can draw its claws back into its paws.

14:45 A cat spends only one third of its life awake.

14:46 'Biannual' means twice a year. 'Biennial' means every two years.

14:47 The name for a group of barrage balloons is a 'balloon barrage'.

14:48 Big Ben is named after an eighteenth-century politician who weighed 158 kilograms.

14:49 Tapioca comes from America.

14:50 It is often the lioness who does most of the killing of prey, then the male comes and eats the 'lion's share'.

14:51 There is only one King and Queen termite in a nest, the other million or so are their children.

14:52 There are 1200 varieties of buttercup.

14:53 A Canadian tattooist had 4831 tattoos on his body.

14:54 The button was originally developed as a means of decoration.

14:55 The earth travels one and a half million miles a day.

14:56 A young hawk is called an 'eyas'.

14:57 Only monkeys from the American continent can hang by their tails. Asian and African monkeys cannot.

14:58 Male mosquitos are vegetarians, it is only females that bite.

14:59 We have approximately 100,000 hairs on our head.

15:00 George V collected 325 albums full of stamps.

15:01 Charles I was only 4 feet 7 inches tall.

15:02 Julius Caesar's autograph has been valued at over one million pounds.

15:03 The armistice at the end of the First World War was signed on the eleventh hour of the eleventh day of the eleventh month in 1918.

15:04 Skin grafts can only be taken from other parts of your body or from an identical twin.

15:05 Our muscles only work by pulling, they never push.

15:06 Film awards given during the war were made of wood to conserve metal.

15:07 An egg will bounce if soaked in vinegar.

15:08 Burning rubber and cork are the most difficult fires to put out.

15:09 In New Zealand there is a place called 'Doubtful Sound'.

15:10 Madame de Pompadour was the first person in France to keep a goldfish.

15:11 The amount of heat generated by a human being living on a normal western daily diet is about the same as that produced by a 120-watt light bulb.

`15:12` There is a breed of cow called 'Why'.

`15:13` Hungary is the largest exporter of hippopotamuses in the world.

`15:14` An omelette large enough to feed twelve men can be made from one ostrich egg.

`15:15` A fully grown human brain weighs three pounds.

`15:16` Handel composed a Mass when he was thirteen.

`15:17` The leaves of young dandelions are delicious in salads.

`15:18` When Archbishop Cranmer was burnt his heart was found intact among the ashes.

`15:19` April Fools' Day is called Fish Day in France.

`15:20` The duck-billed platypus is the only mammal with poisonous glands.

`15:21` The blood of a lobster is blue.

`15:22` The Queen on a playing card was originally the wife of Henry VII.

`15:23` Cucumbers and tomatoes are actually fruits, not vegetables.

`15:24` Rhubarb is a vegetable, not a fruit.

`15:25` A sturgeon caught in British waters is the property of the Queen.

`15:26` Every spring the level of the oceans in the Northern Hemisphere falls 20 cms.

`15:27` In Germany there are nearly 2000 varieties of sausage.

`15:28` Sea horses make a clicking noise.

`15:29` Artificial eyes were sold as long ago as 1734.

`15:30` The original Cinderella's slippers were fur, not glass.

`15:31` Bulls are colourblind.

`15:32` On 14th January 1955, Big Ben in London was stopped by a lump of snow.

`15:33` The foot of a fly is sticky, thus enabling it to walk on the ceiling.

`15:34` The contents of a brown egg are exactly the same as those of a white egg.

15:35 Fishes are able to make noises audible to each other.

15:36 Mary Queen of Scots was made Queen when she was only six days old.

15:37 India is the second largest producer of rice in the world.

15:38 Fireflies and glow-worms are not worms or flies – they are beetles.

15:39 In the eighteenth century criminals were used to test smallpox vaccinations.

15:40 The Swordbill humming-bird has a bill longer than its own body.

15:41 Mount Athos in Greece is inhabited entirely by monks.

15:42 Mosquitos prefer to bite people with fair hair.

15:43 Glasgow, Dublin and Aberdeen were popular first names in nineteenth-century America.

15:44 British people spend more money on pet food than baby food.

15:45 There are approximately 200 million left-handed people in the world.

15:46 Old fish croak an octave higher than young ones.

15:47 Hair that has grown cannot turn white.

15:48 In 1971, astronaut Allan Shepherd played golf on the moon.

15:49 The most frequently used letter in the English language is 'E'.

15:50 The Sargasso Sea is so polluted that there is more oil on the surface than seaweed.

15:51 The common house fly carries at least thirty different diseases which a man can catch.

15:52 The world's highest waterfall is the Angel Falls in Venezuela.

15:53 Nearly half the heat that your body loses is through the top of your head – which is why we wear hats.

15:54 Benjamin Franklin was the youngest son of a youngest son of a youngest son of a youngest son.

15:55 The great actress Sarah Bernhardt played the role of Juliet when she was over seventy.

15:56 If a man had wings like a bird he would need a breast-bone two metres long to hold all the muscles he would require to fly.

15:57 Tongue prints are as unique as finger prints.

15:58 Pope Adrian IV was the only English Pope.

15:59 King John did not sign the Magna Carta – he could not write.

16:00 The first recorded Christmas tree was in 1605.

16:01 Samuel Taylor Coleridge wrote:
'Swans sing before they die – 'twere no bad thing
Should certain persons die before they sing.'

16:02 Swans do not sing before they die – they are mute, apart from the odd croaking sound.

16:03 The human heart is not to the right or left of our bodies but in the centre.

16:04 Madame Tussaud's in London receives at least two letters a week from people who want to sleep in the Chamber of Horrors!

16:05 In 1800 a steeplejack fell 120 feet from a church steeple without being hurt.

16:06 Threadneedle Street in London used to be called 'Pig Street'.

16:07 There is a town called Duffel in Holland where Duffel coats were originally made.

16:08 Romans had their hair singed, not cut.

16:09 If all the stars in the Milky Way had names it would take 4000 years to say them all – at the rate of one name per second!

16:10 The 'Goose Step' which we associate with Germany was an English invention.

16:11 During the sixteenth century it was against the law for Japanese people to leave Japan.

16:12 Giuseppe de Mai was born with two hearts.

16:13 The earth rotates at a speed of 29 kilometres a minute.

16:14 Mistletoe feeds on the tree on which it is growing and eventually kills it.

16:15 'Squirrel' is a Greek word meaning 'shadow tail'.

16:16 King Solomon had 700 wives.

16:17 The word 'lollipop' was first used in 1792.

16:18 At a convent in Germany in the fifteenth century, nuns suddenly began biting each other for no apparent reason!

16:19 Jack O'Leary of California had hiccups for eight years.

16:20 In 1882 a camera like a gun was made in France.

16:21 A tower in Aluges Mortes in France has walls 23 feet thick.

16:22 In California redwood trees grow to over 350 feet in height.

16:23 The energy spent in ten minutes of a hurricane is equal to all the energy of the world's nuclear stock piles.

16:24 The tower of the parish church in Farnborough, Kent, is the fifth to be built – one caught fire in 1688, the other three blew down.

16:25 More than 50,000 earthquakes take place every year – most of them are so slight that they are not even noticed.

16:26 The light that reaches us from the Crab Nebula left there when the civilisation of ancient Egypt was at its height.

16:27 The fastest crossing of the Atlantic by boat is 3 days, 10 hours and 40 minutes.

16:28
$33 \times 3367 = 111,111$
$66 \times 3367 = 222,222$
$99 \times 3367 = 333,333$ and so on until
$297 \times 3367 = 999,999$

16:29 The wandering albatross has a wing span that is roughly twice as long as the arm span of an average-sized man.

16:30 Flies generally prefer to breed in the centre of a room.

16:31 Mensen Erst, a Norwegian, ran from Paris to Moscow in two weeks – swimming across thirteen large rivers to get there.

16:32 There is no reference in the Bible to an apple.

16:33 The water pressure inside every onion cell would be enough to explode a steam engine.

16:34 Prime Minister Disraeli slept with the legs of his bed in bowls of salt water to ward off evil spirits.

16:35 The star nearest to the earth, with the exception of the sun, *Proxima Centauri*, is 24,800,000,000,000 miles away.

16:36 Footballer Peter Lorimer has kicked a football 120.54 kilometres an hour.

16:37 If the monument that was built to commemorate the Great Fire of London were to fall over in an easterly direction, the top would land exactly where the fire started in Pudding Lane.

16:38 No one knows exactly when Jesus Christ was born, but it was sometime between the year 8 BC and the year 6 AD.

16:39 In 1776 a woman who was fond of sneezing, called Margaret Thompson, was buried in a coffin full of snuff.

16:40 A golfer can hit a golf ball through a telephone directory and 100 yards beyond.

16:41 Every verse of psalm 136 ends with the same words.

16:42 Water pressure in the ocean is so great that if you dropped a glass bottle out of a ship it would be broken before it hit the bottom.

16:43 Louis XIV only took four baths in his lifetime.

16:44 Doctors used to carry stethoscopes under their top hats.

16:45 Adrienne Cuyot of Belgium was married fifty-three times.

16:46 Dogs' teeth were used for money until this century in the Solomon Islands.

16:47 Haj Ahmel had 385 wives, all from different parts of the world so that they could not communicate with each other.

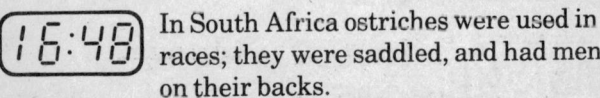

16:48 In South Africa ostriches were used in races; they were saddled, and had men on their backs.

16:49 Babies are six times more active when awake than when asleep.

16:50 Giraffes show affection for each other by pressing their necks together.

16:51 The first aeroplanes were modelled on box kites.

16:52 More than half the world's silver is used in photography and mirror manufacture.

16:53 Newspapers are full of carbohydrates, and therefore edible in small quantities.

16:54 It used to be believed that toads caused warts. South Americans believed toads cured warts.

16:55 In Pakistan there is an area six miles square that contains one million graves.

16:56 In 1907 a prisoner escaped from a German gaol by chewing through the wooden bars.

16:57 Twenty-three per cent of the world's population speak Chinese.

16:58 The Romans used concrete.

16:59 The poet Byron's last words were, 'Goodnight'.

17:00 When the cathedral at Amiens, in France was completed in the Middle Ages, it was possible for everyone who lived in the city, about 10,000 people, to fit inside.

17:01 There are as many molecules of water in a teaspoon of water as there are teaspoons of water in the Atlantic Ocean.

17:02 Only two types of mice are found in Ireland.

17:03 When Mohammed Ali was ruler of Egypt he had two complete armies of one-eyed men.

17:04 As recently as the early nineteenth century only half the population of England ate meat.

17:05 It used to be general practice for blacksmiths to set broken bones.

17:06 Until the tenth century AD there was no city in Europe with a population of more than 400,000 people.

17:07 Cement can be made stronger by adding sugar.

17:08 The living are outnumbered by the dead thirty to one.

17:09 A new-born kangaroo is 2.5 cm long.

17:10 In the sixteenth century a man was born in China with transparent flesh.

17:11 The English language is very similar to Egyptian.

17:12 In the early days of firearms guns took so long to load that a skilled bowman was twelve times more efficient in battle than a man armed with a gun.

17:13 In Spain people fix palm leaves to their roofs in the belief that they will protect them from lightning.

17:14 It was once law that if a man survived three attempts to hang him he was freed.

17:15 When George IV was crowned in July 1821 his train was 32 feet long.

17:16 The average height of a man is considered to be 5 feet 9 inches.

17:17 Ice-cream was invented in 1620.

17:18 There are nearly 450 mosques in Istanbul.

17:19 Buttermilk does not contain any butter.

17:20 The commonest tree in the world is the Larch.

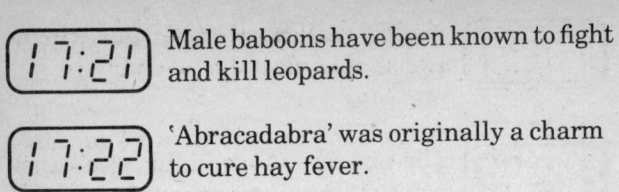 Male baboons have been known to fight and kill leopards.

`17:22` 'Abracadabra' was originally a charm to cure hay fever.

`17:23` Every clown has his own special face make-up that nobody can copy.

`17:24` In 1790, Ah Kwei of China had 135 living great-great-great-great-great-great-great-great grandchildren.

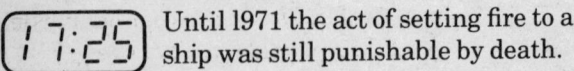 Until 1971 the act of setting fire to a ship was still punishable by death.

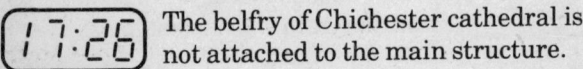 The belfry of Chichester cathedral is not attached to the main structure.

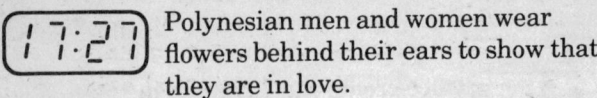 Polynesian men and women wear flowers behind their ears to show that they are in love.

`17:28` Horseshoes came into use over 2000 years ago.

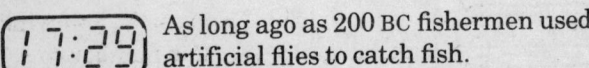 As long ago as 200 BC fishermen used artificial flies to catch fish.

`17:30` There are over five million sheep in Wales.

`17:31` No peer is allowed to wear gloves in the House of Lords if the sovereign is present.

`17:32` The Empire State building was struck by lightning sixty-eight times in the first ten years that it was built.

`17:33` During her lifetime, Queen Victoria never allowed the Royal train to travel at more than 30 miles per hour.

`17:34` In 1901 the train carrying Queen Victoria's body to Windsor travelled at speeds of up to 95 miles per hour. The great lady would not have been amused.

`17:35` Filipinos wait until an egg is just about to hatch before they cook it.

`17:36` The oldest account of a chimney describes one in Venice in 1347.

`17:37` Queen bees may lay as many as 3000 eggs in one day.

`17:38` While a man sleeps for eight hours his body burns up the same number of calories as it would if he had been running for 52 minutes.

`17:39` Potato crisps were invented by the American Indians.

`17:40` The amoeba consumes its food by wrapping its body around it.

`17:41` You can tell if a man is left- or right-handed by watching which leg he puts first into his trousers.

`17:42` We would die more quickly from lack of sleep than lack of food.

`17:43` Eighty per cent of all the species of the freshwater fish on earth are found in the Amazon.

`17:44` In 1940 a concert was given to monkeys in a Philadelphia zoo.

`17:45` The first aerial photograph was taken during the American Civil War, from a balloon.

`17:46` One of the shortest poems written:
Adam
Had 'em.

`17:47` Earwigs are vegetarians and are unlikely to enter your ears.

`17:48` President Roosevelt used to have an ink-well made from the hollowed-out foot of a rhinoceros.

`17:49` The foot of Mont Blanc is in Italy, but the summit is in France.

17:50 A hotel in Tokyo once had a solid gold bath.

17:51 Gold is indestructible.

17:52 Scientists have found that mice prefer women to men.

17:53 A dentist once grew a dwarf conifer tree in an extracted tooth.

17:54 Twenty thousand years ago men on a hunt drank blood.

17:55 Baobab trees found in the tropics have trunks thirty feet in diameter.

17:56 A snake has no eyelid.

17:57 At least thirty-one different shapes of UFO have been sighted in the world.

17:58 People used to swallow live frogs to clear out their systems.

17:59 When he was only seven years old, the Russian composer Sergei Prokofiev wrote an opera called *The Giant*.

18:00 George IV once rode from London to Brighton and back in ten hours.

18:01 Edward VII used to weigh his guests after week-ends at Sandringham to make sure that they had eaten well.

18:02 Thirteen million working days are lost each year in Britain due to backache.

18:03 Clams on the Malayan coast are large enough to eat a man.

18:04 The state of Indonesia is made up of 13,000 islands.

18:05 In 1812 an American Colonel walked from St Louis to Leningrad.

18:06 One beehive can make up to one kilo of honey a day, which will involve five million bee journeys to flowers.

18:07 Russia produces enough oil annually to drive an average car to the sun and back 46,000 times.

18:08 Twelve cars are manufactured every minute in the USA.

18:09 The coronation ceremony for English monarchs is practically the same as in the year 973.

18:10 Each of us has a set of muscles in our body that we no longer use. Originally they were meant to move our ears.

18:11 In a boxing match in 1912, the boxers simultaneously knocked each other out.

18:12 Spencer Perceval was the only British Prime Minister to be murdered. He was shot in the House of Commons the 11th May 1921.

18:13 The famous author George Eliot was in fact a woman.

18:14 Salisbury Cathedral was once taken down piece by piece and rebuilt on its present site – it took forty years.

18:15 In June 1785 a law was passed in France that all handkerchiefs should be square.

18:16 By 1985 there will be 200 billion telephones in the world.

18:17 A falcon can fly at a speed of 290 kilometres per hour.

18:18 The longest unbroken apple peel is 30 metres long and took eight hours to peel.

18:19 In Tahiti bands of zinc are put around the bottom of coconut trees to prevent rats from climbing up them.

18:20 Ostrich feather fans found in the tomb of Tutankhamun were still intact after 3000 years.

18:21 The youngest stars in the galaxy were born sixty million years ago.

18:22 The USSR spreads over such a wide area that it covers seven time zones.

18:23 Pepi II was Pharoah in Egypt for ninety-four years.

18:24 Since 1496 there have been only 233 war-free years.

18:25 A zebra has white stripes, not black ones.

18:26 The Dead Sea is so salty that it is impossible to sink.

18:27 Scientists estimate that at its centre the sun has a density of over one hundred times that of water.

18:28 Turkish baths were devised by the Romans.

18:29 In Mexico three people once became president on one day.

18:30 King George VI once played tennis in the Wimbledon Championships.

18:31 William Shakespeare had red hair.

18:32 A dog has forty-two teeth.

18:33 Twenty-four sheets of paper are called a 'quire'.

18:34 A baby herring is called a 'fry'.

18:35 Water boils at a temperature of 212 degrees fahrenheit.

18:36 The winter in 1641 was so cold that the Black Sea froze over.

18:37 Rubber is the sap of a tropical tree.

18:38 In 1790 there were many hoax earthquake scares, causing fear and panic in the city of London.

18:39 In Charles Kingsley's book *The Water Babies* there is a character called Mrs Doasyouwouldbedoneby.

18:40 Some golf balls have castor oil inside them.

18:41 A tightrope walker is called a 'funambulist'.

`18:42` William Gladstone became Prime Minister four times.

`18:43` Women were not allowed to vote until 1918.

`18:44` A group of kittens is called a 'kindle'.

`18:45` The correct name for bellringing is 'campanology'.

`18:46` The highest mountain in the world is Mount Everest: it is 29,141 feet.

`18:47` The first escalator in a London shop was installed in Harrods in 1898.

`18:48` The first traffic lights in London were set up outside the Houses of Parliament in 1868. They were red and green only.

`18:49` In 1920 two small girls were found in a wolf's den in India, and appeared to have been reared by the wolves.

`18:50` The St Edward's crown, worn by the Queen at her coronation, has over 400 precious stones in it.

`18:51` The sovereign who reigned for longest was Queen Victoria, who was on the throne for sixty-four years.

18:52 The Union Jack is made up from three crosses – those of St George, St Andrew and St Patrick.

18:53 Nearly one hemisphere of the earth's surface is taken up by the Pacific Ocean.

18:54 In 1878 the Queen of Madagascar was buried in a coffin of 30,000 silver coins riveted together.

18:55 Lord's cricket ground was originally in Dorset Square.

18:56 Man is the only animal that sleeps on its back.

18:57 At the court of Louis XIV only the King and Queen were allowed to sit on armchairs.

18:58 Charles II was the first British Monarch to go to a theatre.

18:59 The brain of Neanderthal man was approximately one and a half inches bigger than ours.

19:00 Nero hoped to improve his singing voice by eating leeks.

19:01 A man named Al Cohol was once charged with drunkenness.

`19:02` The human brain uses the same power as a ten-watt electric bulb.

`19:03` Mayflies live only a few hours after they are hatched.

`19:04` The Great Wall of China is one of the few man-made objects visible from the moon.

`19:05` The most widely-used drug on earth is a tranquilliser called 'Valium'.

`19:06` There is a street in Canada that is nearly 1,900 kilometres in length.

`19:07` Three 25-watt light bulbs produce less light than one 75-watt bulb.

`19:08` The first book by the Brontë sisters sold two copies in its first year of publication. It was a joint volume of poems which cost the three sisters fifty pounds to be published.

`19:09` There is a goose in Hawaii called a 'Ne-Ne'.

`19:10` At the battle of Copenhagen in 1801 Nelson put his telescope up to his blind eye to avoid reading a message which he did not want to follow. As a result he won a glorious victory.

19:11 The Marquis of Anglesey had his leg amputated during the Battle of Waterloo – the leg was given a full military funeral.

19:12 There is a bird in Hawaii called the 'O-O'.

19:13 A cure in France for insomnia was to eat an apple at 7.00 am under the Arc de Triomph.

19:14 When Princess Anne married in 1973 her wedding bouquet contained a sprig of myrtle grown from a myrtle used in Queen Victoria's wedding bouquet.

19:15 Rubber is used in the manufacture of bubble gum.

19:16 Napoleon was a keen player of solitaire.

19:17 The first elephant was not much bigger than a modern pig.

19:18 The largest living animal without a backbone is the giant squid.

19:19 Ostriches can swim.

19:20 Desert snails sometimes remain sleeping in their shells for over a year.

`19:21` Alligators and humans can only hear notes with up to 4000 vibrations a second.

`19:22` It is impossible to sneeze with your eyes open.

`19:23` There is a market in Holland that sells nothing but cheese.

`19:24` In 1685 mail moved around Britain at a rate of five miles per hour.

`19:25` On the eve of Alexander the Great's expedition to Asia, a statue of Orpheus is said to have sweated for several days.

`19:26` Early graves were constructed with the shoulder blades of prehistoric animals.

`19:27` From the bottom of a well it is possible to see stars even in daylight.

`19:28` Liquid fuel was first used in a rocket in 1948.

`19:29` Packaged frozen foods were invented by Clarence Birdseye.

`19:30` Milk was first served with coffee in Vienna in 1683.

19:31 Mozart died of typhoid fever in 1791, but was convinced that he was being poisoned.

19:32 The human stomach can stretch to hold two pints of liquid.

19:33 George Washington was the first man to wear false teeth – they were made from wood.

19:34 The human body contains enough phosphorus to make 2000 matches.

19:35 The first great woman recorded in history is Queen Hatsheput who ruled ancient Egypt from 1511 to 1480 BC.

19:36 In 1890, 180,000 mummified cats were auctioned in Liverpool.

19:37 The first member of our Royal family to be interviewed on television was Prince Philip in 1961.

19:38 Baron Dominique Larry, Napoleon's surgeon, could amputate a man's leg in fourteen seconds.

19:39 There is no reference to a duck in the Old Testament.

19:40 The practice of 'giving away the bride' at a wedding dates back to earlier times when it used to be done for money.

19:41 Shooting stars are not stars but meteors.

19:42 In Indiana, USA, it is illegal to travel on a bus within four hours of eating garlic.

19:43 Beetles have been kept for up to two years without food – living on their own discarded skins.

19:44 In 1963 a star was discovered that is a million million times brighter than the sun. It does not affect us because we are 1.5 billion light years away.

19:45 Near Kiama, in New South Wales, there is a rock formation that looks like a cathedral.

19:46 In Iceland families do not have surnames.

19:47 As light takes 400 years to reach us from a star, it is possible that many of the stars we see may not have existed for 300 years.

19:48 Venus is our closest neighbour – 25 million miles away.

19:49 In 1831, an Italian operatic tenor strained so hard to get a note that he dislocated his collar bone.

19:50 Brakes did not become a standard feature on cars until the 1920s.

19:51 With the advent of the cartoon character 'Popeye' the amount of land used to grow spinach in America was increased twenty-one times.

19:52 As late as 1675 it was believed that mermaids were among the animals on Noah's ark.

19:53 Seaweed is used in the manufacture of toothpaste and ice-cream.

19:54 It can take as long as 500 days to drill an oil well five miles deep, and that's with the drill working twenty-four hours a day for seven days a week.

19:55 In 1976 one in ten men died of lung cancer in Britain.

19:56 Zacharius Jansen invented a microscope in 1590.

| `19:57` | The first record of a murder trial is of one held in 1700 BC. |

| `19:58` | Redheads have fewer hairs on their heads than people with blonde hair. |

| `19:59` | The chalk used on blackboards is made from plaster of paris. |

| `20:00` | Man only uses about four per cent of the plants that grow on earth. |

| `20:01` | The official name for a wren is 'Troglodytes troglodytes'. |

| `20:02` | In 1886 a driverless engine ran from Petworth to Horsham in Surrey before being stopped. |

| `20:03` | A mouse cannot tell one human face from another at a range of two metres. |

| `20:04` | John Bunyan wrote *Pilgrim's Progress* whilst serving a twelve-year prison sentence. |

| `20:05` | During the winter the South Pole is nearer to the sun than any other part of the earth. |

| `20:06` | Most of what we call tastes are actually smells. |

20:07 Pierre Labellière had such a dislike of the world that when he died he was buried upside down.

20:08 1858 was a very hot summer, causing the Thames in London to stink!

20:09 An albatross can fly all day and not flap its wings once.

20:10 Pluto is the coldest planet in the solar system.

20:11 In Africa peanuts are ground and made into a cake.

20:12 A 15-inch-long Scottish terrier in Manchester once swallowed a knitting needle – 12 inches long!

20:13 In Mexico there is a pyramid over 200 feet high - held together by sand, clay, and ground corn.

20:14 In Zimbabwe there are 620 different species of bird.

20:15 On old watches with Roman numerals the number 4 is expressed not as IV but as IIII, so as not to confuse it with VI.

20:16 Elephant hunters train other elephants to help them trap their prey.

20:17 The only way an elephant can be killed with a normal hunting rifle is to shoot it in the eye or just above the trunk.

20:18 The area drained by the mighty river Amazon in South America is almost as big as the USA.

20:19 Women over the age of twenty-five suffer far more illnesses than men do.

20:20 About 1000 tons of meteor dust fall on the earth every day.

20:21 It would be possible for a person to speak his entire vocabulary in half an hour.

20:22 An owl is the only bird capable of looking at an object with both eyes at the same time.

20:23 In 1901 a man was fined in Cardiff for speeding. He was travelling at ten miles per hour.

20:24 In April 1884 there was an earthquake in East Anglia which killed four people.

20:25 A clock loses weight as it unwinds itself.

`20:26` The walls of Babylon were 26 metres thick.

`20:27` In one season ten water hyacinths can increase sixty thousand times to form a mat an acre in size.

`20:28` The Colosseum in Rome staged entertainment for over 400 years.

`20:29` There have only been three left-handed monarchs in England – James I, Queen Victoria, and George IV.

`20:30` Man is the only animal that blushes – or needs to!

`20:31` The odds against a mother having quadruplets are about one in 600,000.

`20:32` The final words of the English critic Lytton Strachey were, 'If this is dying, I don't think much of it.'

`20:33` The building of wheeled transport is 1000 years older than the building of roads.

`20:34` Before the First World War it was more common for men to diet than ladies.

20:35 A kiss has been medically described as, 'the anatomical juxtaposition of two orbicularis oris muscles in a state of contraction'.

20:36 The flower of the Firecracker Tree that grows in Hawaii opens with a loud bang.

20:37 There is a water-raising song called the 'chadouf' which has been sung on the banks of the Nile for about 5000 years.

20:38 A blind and handicapped Scotsman called William McPherson learnt to read with his tongue.

20:39 Virtually all fish caught in the world come from only ten per cent of the waters.

20:40 A seventeenth-century doctor claimed that the earth was created at 9.00 am on 23rd October 4004 BC.

20:41 Most Elizabethan stories were written to be read aloud.

20:42 One of the best natural oils in the world is castor oil. Even jet aircraft have a dose occasionally.

20:43 Over half the tin cans made in the world are used in the USA.

20:44 Half the area of the Netherlands lies below sea level.

20:45 A guinea-pig is a rodent, not a pig.

20:46 Shakespeare mentioned America in his play 'A Comedy of Errors'.

20:47 A swarm of locusts over the Red Sea in 1889 covered an area of 5180 square kilometres.

20:48 The word 'tragedy' comes from the Greek words meaning 'goat song'.

20:49 Queen Victoria lived four days longer than the longest reigning king, George III.

20:50 The forests of the Amazon provide forty per cent of the world's oxygen.

20:51 One of the most effective lobster baits is a brick soaked in paraffin.

20:52 Koala bears get their name from the Aborigine meaning 'no drink'.

20:53 Buffalo Bill actually hunted bison.

20:54 On the Panama Canal you can watch the sun rise over the Pacific and set in the Atlantic.

20:55 The United States mint once stamped 'In Gold we Trust' on coins by mistake, instead of 'In God we Trust'.

20:56 The liver of a shark can represent ten per cent of its body weight.

20:57 In the nineteenth century it was believed that chewing gum would stick your intestines together.

20:58 Submarines cannot remain still in water, they have to move up or down.

20:59 The volcano, Mount Fuji, in Japan is so light at the summit that it moves in the wind.

21:00 More hunters have been killed by the buffalo than by any other wild animal.

21:01 In 1971 in Argentina a cow was killed when it lay down on a railway track. While waiting for the train to be repaired the passengers ate the cow!

21:02 1928 saw the death of the Polish character, Reb Frommer, who, after a self-imposed penance, did not speak for thirty years.

21:03 All the ants that work so hard in ant armies are female.

21:04 Switzerland never goes to war, but has an army of 350,000 men.

21:05 The word 'school' comes from a Greek word meaning 'leisure'.

21:06 Attila the Hun was a dwarf.

21:07 The Chinese used rockets in 1232.

21:08 Julius Caesar suffered from epileptic fits.

21:09 There are 2000 species of parsley.

21:10 Romans used a paste of chalk and vinegar as a deodorant.

21:11 Queen Elizabeth I took a bath once a month.

21:12 The largest village green is at Hallingbury in Essex and is 62¾ acres.

21:13 A kipper is a dried, cured herring.

21:14 Margarine is named after the Greek word for 'pearl'.

21:15 The last Welsh-born Prince of Wales was Llewelyn, who died in 1282.

21:16 The largest lake in England is Lake Windermere, which is 5.7 square miles.

21:17 England covers an area of 50,332 square miles and has a population of approximately 45,870,062.

21:18 The largest bell in Britain is in St Paul's Cathedral. It weighs 16¾ quarter tons.

21:19 The pneumatic tyre was first invented in 1888.

21:20 The church at Chesterfield is famous because it has a crooked spire.

21:21 Captain James Cook spent six months mapping the coastline of New Zealand in 1769.

21:22 Britain's youngest Prime Minister was William Pitt the Younger, who was aged just twenty-four.

21:23 Mary Queen of Scots had three husbands.

21:24 The author Samuel Butler wrote a famous book called *Erewhon* – which is an anagram of 'nowhere'.

21:25 Neither the dormouse nor the nightingale are found in Ireland.

21:26 There are fifty-seven different species of land mammal living in the British Isles.

21:27 The sparrow and the blackbird are the most common birds – there are about ten million of each in this country.

21:28 At Great Yarmouth in Norfolk there is a second Nelson's Column.

21:29 In Somerset there is a place called 'Huish Episcopi'.

21:30 The first penny post was started in 1680, and at the same time the postmark was invented.

21:31 Meat was the last item to be freed from rationing, after the war, in 1954.

21:32 The correct medical term for a common cold is 'acute nasopharyngitis'.

21:33 High tides on the sea are on average 12 hours and 25 minutes apart.

21:34 A portrait painted by the artist Sir Joshua Reynolds showed a man with a hat on his head – and another under his arm.

21:35 In twelve years between 1920 and 1932 the Finnish runner Paave Nurmi won nine gold medals at the Olympic Games and broke twenty world records.

21:36 The bones of our skeleton account for only 20 per cent of our total body weight.

21:37 The traffic problem got so bad in ancient Rome that Julius Caesar had to ban all vehicles from the city during the day.

21:38 Some of the cells of our body are so small that 200,000 would fit on a pin head.

21:39 In pagan times girls used to tie holly on to their beds to save themselves from turning into witches.

21:40 In 1877 Dr Alpheus Meyers invented a 'Tapeworm Trap', which was similar to a mousetrap and was swallowed to try and catch the worm's head. Instead patients choked to death.

21:41 As recently as 1820 some scientists believed that the Universe was only 6000 years old. Today ideas have changed and the Universe is reckoned to be at least fifteen thousand million years old.

21:42 Medieval Germans used to go to the barbers for a bath as well as a haircut.

21:43 In India, for more than 2000 years, a cow's moo was used as a measure of distance.

21:44 In America there are eight different cities called 'Rome'.

21:45 During the French Revolution a midget was used as a spy and was carried through the enemy lines disguised as a baby.

21:46 Nearly 40 per cent of Russia is covered by forest.

21:47 Many Roman statues were made with detachable heads.

21:48 Richard III and Napoleon were both born with teeth.

21:49 The first road-side petrol pump was installed in 1920.

21:50 Houses were first numbered in London in 1764.

21:51 Henry VIII's second wife, Anne Boleyn, had an extra finger on her left hand.

21:52 Oil from apricots is used in the manufacture of cosmetics.

21:53 Some European cathedrals have foundations that go down for 50 feet underground.

21:54 One gallon of water weighs ten pounds.

21:55 Francis Bacon, an Elizabethan philosopher, tried to freeze a chicken by stuffing it with snow. As a result he caught a chill and died.

21:56 In 1888 in Northern India nearly 250 people were killed by hailstones.

21:57 Zoologically the killer whale is a dolphin.

21:58 Flies take off with a backward jump.

21:59 Spandau Prison in Berlin costs nearly a quarter of a million pounds a year to maintain, and yet contains only one prisoner.

22:00 Paper was made by wasps thousands of years before man.

22:01 In 1060 a coin was made in the shape of a four-leaved clover. Each leaf could be broken off and used separately.

22:02 Napoleon travelled to the Battle of Waterloo in a bullet-proof coach.

22:03 Annie Oakley could shoot a hole in a playing card tossed in the air.

22:04 Ray Cantwell of Oxford, a marathon letter writer, once wrote over 2900 letters in 317 hours.

22:05 The world's most powerful telescope can detect a candle flame 24,000 kilometres away.

22:06 Marlene Raymond a limbo dancer from Canada, once slithered under a flaming bar that was only 15.5 cm above the ground.

22:07 In 1977 Emma Disley climbed Mount Snowdon wearing a pair of stilts.

22:08 Statistics show that more people die through being kicked by donkeys than are involved in flying accidents.

22:09 The energy released by a bolt of lightning is equivalent to that needed to raise an average-sized ship two metres in the air.

22:10 At their closest points the USSR and the USA are just three kilometres apart.

22:11 Boxwood is one of the few woods that sinks in water.

22:12 An egg is 40 per cent heavier when it is laid than just before it hatches.

22:13 Since May 1946 every country in the world has sighted UFOs.

22:14 Alexander the Great had very large helmets made, which were left lying around in the hope that his enemies would think his army was made up of giants.

22:15 The gravity on Jupiter is much greater than Earth's gravity, so if you visited that planet you would weigh a lot more.

22:16 The three-toed sloth disguises itself by allowing its body to be covered by a layer of tiny plants.

22:17 Left-handed playing cards have pips in all four corners.

22:18 The first English Parliament met in 1265.

22:19 Since 1730 there have been forty-nine Prime Ministers in England.

22:20 There is a peak in the Lake District known as 'Dollywaggon Pike'.

22:21 Lord Barrymore, born 1769, had £1000 a year pocket money while still at school.

22:22 In 1817, Lady Luttrell incurred debts amounting to £50,000, and after release from prison was found guilty of picking pockets and was sentenced to six months of sweeping the streets – chained to a wheelbarrow.

22:23 Bank notes with a value of one thousand pounds each were still in circulation until the Second World War.

22:24 Tests show that girls talk about boys three times more than boys discuss girls.

22:25 Cows lie down in grass to keep a warm, dry patch if it is going to rain.

22:26 Cuckoos lay their eggs in other birds' nests. Their eggs are larger, but are frequently similar in colouring to the eggs already there.

22:27 The largest island in the world is Greenland, covering 838,000 square miles.

22:28 Cheese takes 3 hours and 30 minutes to be digested.

22:29 Charles Dickens wrote fourteen major novels.

22:30 Bells were first used in Christian churches in the year 400 AD.

22:31 The expression 'up with the lark' derives from the fact that the lark is one of the first birds to be heard singing in the morning, at approximately 3.28 am.

22:32 Between Jupiter and Mars there are some 500 asteroids, some no larger than five miles in diameter.

22:33 In 1808 two rival Frenchmen fought a duel in hot air balloons. When they fired their shots one missed, while the other hit the balloon, causing it to crash and killing the occupant.

22:34 'Anubus testudineus' is the name of a remarkable fish – not only can it crawl along the ground for a distance of up to one mile, but it is capable of climbing trees!

22:35 A famous Persian law-giver ate nothing but cheese for thirty years.

22:36 In 1894 a cricket match was held in India in which a team of eleven natives with bats played against eleven army officers with umbrellas.

22:37 The sand of Kauai in Hawaii makes a noise like a dog barking when stepped on.

22:38 Mercury, although a liquid, is in fact a metal.

22:39 The ice-flower, the Soldanella, in Switzerland forces its way up through the ice.

22:40 In 1812 a six-year-old American boy, named Zerah Colburn, had remarkable arithmetical skills. When asked to multiply 21,734 by 543 he gave the answer in a few seconds. He arrived at the answer, he said, by multiplying 65,202 by 181, which gave the same answer!

22:41 The oldest Royal family in the world is that of Emperor Hirohito, in Japan, which has maintained an unbroken line for 2600 years.

22:42 An epitaph on a tombstone at Ockham, Surrey, 1736:
The Lord saw good, I was lopping off wood,
>   And down fell from the tree;
I met with a check, and I broke my neck,
>   And so death lopp'd off me!

22:43 During one visit to London at the height of his film popularity, Charlie Chaplin received 73,000 letters in two days.

22:44 Bees have to collect the nectar from about five million flowers to make a pound of comb honey.

22:45 The chemical name for the common salt that we eat is sodium chloride.

22:46 Mustard will remove ink stains, and is good for cleaning silver.

22:47 Misprint in a newspaper:
'Unless the teachers receive a higher salary they may decide to leave their pests . . . .'

22:48 There is no chamois in chamois leather – it is made from the flesh side of sheep skin.

22:49 There are twelve metals heavier than lead.

22:50 In 1804 at Toulouse in France there was a shower of frogs during a storm. Roads and fields were full of the creatures.

22:51 It is always reported that Nero played the fiddle while Rome burned. This is untrue – fiddles had not been invented, and he was fifty miles away at his villa at the time of the fire.

22:52 Leon Avazion once climbed to the top of the Woolworth Building in New York in just nine minutes. The building is fifty-five storeys high and the stairs have 1520 steps.

22:53 The blue whale can survive for six months without eating. During this time it is sustained by the nutrition in its blubber.

22:54 Each feather worn by a Red Indian indicates the number of brave deeds he has done.

22:55 The statesman, Benjamin Franklin, discovered the Gulf Stream, and that the air we breathe out is poisonous.

22:56 Earliest pictures of Santa Claus show him dressed as a bishop.

22:57 Between 1564 and 1814, nine frost fairs were held on the River Thames at Christmas time.

22:58 On Mars you only weigh 38 per cent of your weight on Earth.

22:59 In March 1922 rocks fell from the sky in the town of Chico, California.

23:00 The bud and top two leaves of a tea plant are called a 'flush'. It takes 3500 flushes to make one pound of tea.

23:01 The Japanese consider it unlucky to cut your finger nails before setting out on a journey.

23:02 The meat of a hippopotamus is said to taste like juicy pork.

23:03 The oil in which sardines are packed in a tin is more expensive than the sardines.

23:04 Railway tracks were being used in Alsace mines as early as 1550.

23:05 The entire contents of the first gramophone record:
'Mary had a little lamb'.

23:06 A prehistoric flying animal had a wing span of thirty feet – it was called the pteranodon.

23:07 The thirty-five-ton brontosaurus had a brain weighing only one pound.

23:08 A man could stand on the shell of a hard-boiled ostrich egg without cracking it.

23:09 'Nylon' comes from New York (Ny) and London (Lon) where it was invented.

23:10 A French composer, called Louis Julien, had thirty-six Christian names.

23:11 Underwater walking races used to be held in Tonga.

23:12 The Statue of Liberty was originally erected in France before being taken apart and shipped across the Atlantic to New York, where it was re-assembled.

23:13 The Greek hero Agamemnon was murdered by his wife while in the bath.

23:14 The first photograph of the moon was taken in 1841.

23:15 An anagram of 'punishment' is 'nine thumps'.

23:16 The famous escapologist Houdini was the first solo pilot in Australia.

23:17 The expression 'forlorn hope' comes from the Dutch expression meaning 'lost troop'.

23:18 The large ruby in the Imperial State crown, worn by the Queen, was worn by Henry V at the Battle of Agincourt in 1415.

23:19 It takes a cork tree ten years to grow one layer of cork.

23:20 The number eleven bus from Shepherds Bush to Liverpool Street in London was started in 1866.

23:21 The Reading Room in the British museum has the second largest dome in the world – 140 feet in diameter.

23:22 The highest temperature ever recorded in Britain is 100.5 degrees fahrenheit in 1868 at Tonbridge in Kent.

23:23 The famous French Roquefort cheese is made from sheep's milk.

23:24 The Bible has sold more copies than any other book ever published.

23:25 If your tongue was completely dry you would not be able to taste anything.

23:26 Czar Paul I was so conscious of being bald that anyone who mentioned it was flogged to death.

23:27 The sign for a dollar ($) is a modified version of the symbol stamped on the old Spanish 'pieces of eight'.

23:28 In the sixteenth century men were allowed to beat their wives before 10.00 pm.

23:29 About sixty million years ago the ancestors of the modern horse stood about one foot high.

23:30 There are over 20,000 actors in America, although 16,000 are probably unemployed.

23:31 One of the most popular hobbies in America is collecting buttons. It is quite common to have over 25,000.

`23:32` Buckingham Palace contains 602 rooms.

`23:33` The great Victorian statesman, William Ewart Gladstone, was convinced that the Greeks were colour-blind on the grounds that so few colour words occur in the work of Homer.

`23:34` Queen Rnavalona of Madagascar made it illegal to dream about her.

`23:35` The most powerful acid known in the ancient world was vinegar.

`23:36` In 1160 BC Egyptians building the tomb of Rameses III went on strike for more money.

`23:37` Modern binoculars are more powerful than Galileo's telescope.

`23:38` During the reign of James I it was considered unsuitable to play bowls on a Sunday.

`23:39` Madame Schwartz of Berlin was able to understand speech when words were pronounced backwards – or sdrawkcab!

`23:40` Solar energy was used as early as 1615.

23:41 Cotton was first brought to England at the beginning of the seventh century AD.

23:42 In Hammerfest in Norway, from 18th November to 23rd January the sun never comes above the horizon: it is dark twenty-four hours a day.

23:43 It takes three miles of yarn to make a pair of tights.

23:44 In 1730, Frederick William I, King of Prussia, wanted a cake large enough to feed his army of 30,000 men. It contained 5000 eggs, one ton of butter, 200 gallons of milk and 36 bushels of flour. The resulting cake was 54 feet long, 24 feet wide, and almost 2 feet high.

23:45 The loudest band in the world is called 'Deep Purple'. Three girls were knocked unconscious when they climbed into one of the band's speakers at a concert. The sound is seventeen times lounder than a jet plane flying at 300 metres would be.

23:46 The silk worm is a caterpillar.

23:47 Live toads have been found inside solid lumps of rock.

23:48 Termites can produce substances that can rust metal, burn lead, and disintegrate glass.

23:49 More UFOs are sighted when Mars is nearest the Earth than at any other time.

23:50 The composer Beethoven stimulated his brain by pouring iced water over his head.

23:51 Shakespeare's daughter could not read or write.

23:52 September 15th is fine in England six years out of seven.

23:53 Michael Williams of Illinois spent 60 hours under a shower.

23:54 The white-throated wood rat can run over cactus needles.

23:55 'Bird' in the Middle Ages meant 'woman' or 'damsel'.

23:56 James A. Garfield, a president of America, could write Greek with one hand while at the same time write Latin with the other.

23:57 Beavers can build dams as long as 15 meters.

`23:58` The longest stroke of lightning measured was 32km long.

`23:59` The largest bronze statue in the world is a statue of Buddha in Japan that weighs 452 tons.

On the following pages you will find details of other exciting books from Sparrow.

THE SPARROW BOOK OF RECORD-BREAKERS
Pamela Cleaver

Children have flown planes in the RAF, ridden in cavalry charges and formed an army in which the eldest soldier was twelve years old. A young boy was used as a spy in World War Two, and the youngest author to have a book published was only four and a half years old.

And that is only the beginning . . .

85p

THE COMPLETE PRACTICAL JOKER

Peter Eldin

Have you ever wished that April Fools Day could last all year long?

Have you ever longed to frighten your little sister, get out of the washing up, or drive your friends crazy – without getting into trouble?

Then the book you've been waiting for is here. Confuse your parents, bewilder your teachers, amuse your friends and stay out of trouble with this harmless, but devious book.

95p

A GHOST HUNTER'S HANDBOOK

Peter Underwood

Long-time ghost expert and hunter, Peter Underwood, tells children all they need to know about ghosts, their habits and habitats. Peter Underwood, who is president of the Ghost Club and copyright holder of the only known photograph of a ghost, has written several books on ghosts for adults, but this is his first book on the subject for children. Serious in approach, it covers everything from how to find a ghost to information on ghosts that have been found in all parts of the world, and includes a section on famous ghosts and haunted houses that can be visited.

85p

THERESE BIRCH'S
JELLYBONE GRAFFITI BOOK

For the first time – a collection of the best in graffiti, compiled
by children for children.

Preserve wildlife – pickle a duck

Work fascinates me – I can sit and look at it for hours

Humpty Dumpty was pushed

Take an astronaut to launch

85p

TIME BANDITS

Charles Alverson

Now a major film

Here one minute . . . there the next, from the Napoleonic
Wars to Sherwood Forest, from Agamemnon's Greece to the
deck of the doomed *Titanic*, a band of greedy dwarfs race
through history. They are immortal yet human, timeless but
always late, capable of inter-cosmic travel yet unable to tie
their own shoelaces. Stealing in one century and hiding out in
another, they are the most extraordinary gang ever let loose
on this or any other universe.

They are the Time Bandits.

95p

The Sparrow Bookshop

Sparrow has a whole nestful of exciting books that are available in bookshops or that you can order by post through the Sparrow Bookshop. Just complete the form below and enclose the money due and the books will be sent to you at home.

☐	POEMS TO MAKE YOU LAUGH	ed. Tom Baker	95p
☐	THE SPUDDY	Lillian Beckwith	85p
☐	THE JELLYBONE GRAFFITI BOOK	Terese Birch	85p
☐	THE CARAVAN FAMILY	Enid Blyton	70p
☐	THE SPARROW BOOK OF RECORD BREAKERS	Pamela Cleaver	85p
☐	MIDSHIPMAN BOLITHO	Alexander Kent	80p
☐	THE PONY SEEKERS	Diana Pullein-Thompson	85p
☐	WORZEL GUMMIDGE AND THE TREASURE SHIP	Barbara E. Todd	95p

Picture books

☐	IF MICE COULD FLY	John Cameron	£1.25
☐	NOT NOW, BERNARD	David McKee	£1.25
☐	K9 AND THE TIME TRAP	David Martin	65p
☐	EMERGENCY MOUSE	Ralph Steadman and Bernard Stone	£1.35

Total plus postage

And if you would like to hear more about our forthcoming books, write to the address below for the Sparrow News.

SPARROW BOOKS, BOOKSERVICE BY POST, PO BOX 29, DOUGLAS, ISLE OF MAN, BRITISH ISLES

Please enclose a cheque or postal order made out to Arrow Books Limited for the amount due including 8p per book for postage and packing for orders within the UK and 10p for overseas orders.

Please print clearly

NAME _____

ADDRESS _____

_____

Whilst every effort is made to keep prices down and popular books in print, Arrow Books cannot guarantee that prices will be the same as those advertised here or that the books will be available.